LEADERSHIP LESSONS OF ABRAHAM LINCOLN

LEADERSHIP LESSONS OF ABRAHAM LINCOLN

Strategies, Advice, and Words
of Wisdom on Leadership,
Responsibility, and Power

ABRAHAM LINCOLN

Edited with introductions by
Meg Distinti

Skyhorse Publishing

Skyhorse Publishing books may be purchased in bulk at special discounts for sales promotion, corporate gifts, fund-raising, or educational purposes. Special editions can also be created to specifications. For details, contact the Special Sales Department, Skyhorse Publishing, 307 West 36th Street, 11th Floor, New York, NY 10018 or info@skyhorsepublishing.com.

Skyhorse® and Skyhorse Publishing® are registered trademarks of Skyhorse Publishing, Inc.®, a Delaware corporation.

www.skyhorsepublishing.com

10 9 8 7 6

Library of Congress Cataloging-in-Publication Data

Lincoln, Abraham, 1809-1865
  Leadership lessons of Abraham Lincoln : apply the principles of the sixteenth president to your own work and life / Abraham Lincoln ; edited with introductions by Meg Distinti.
       p. cm.
  Includes bibliographical references and index.
  ISBN 978-1-61608-412-7 (alk. paper)
  1. Leadership--Quotations, maxims, etc. 2. Lincoln, Abraham, 1809-1865--Quotations. 3. Presidents--United States--Biography. I. Distinti, Meg. II. Title.
  HM1261.L553 2011
  352.3'9--dc23
                                2011031729

Printed in the United States of America

To the memory of my Mom,
who loved me enough to drag me
kicking and screaming to the kitchen table
every night to go over my homework.

You taught me the meaning of the words
dedication and leadership.

I will never forgive you for making me
finish all my brussel sprouts.

CONTENTS

LEADERSHIP LESSONS OF ABRAHAM LINCOLN

INTRODUCTION

"Though I now sink out of view, and shall be forgotten, I believe I have made some marks which will tell for the cause of civil liberty long after I am gone."

—*Letter to Anson G. Henry; November 19, 1858*

Abraham Lincoln was born on February 12, 1809, one year before roaming men in suits combed the countryside collecting data for the third census of the United States. The information gathered by those census takers paints a picture of a nation far different from ours today; less than eight million people called themselves citizens and the predominant occupation of almost all individuals in the country was agriculture.

While baby Abraham was learning to crawl, his family and neighbors were busy taming the state of Kentucky, President Madison was enforcing the Embargo Act, and Eli Whitney's Cotton Gin—which had only won its patent in 1807—was revolutionizing the economy of the South. By the time Lincoln died, the U.S. population had more than quadrupled, the industrial age was in full swing, and construction had begun to link the East and West coasts via the transcontinental railroad.

For all that Lincoln was able to preserve, the Union Lincoln saved has become a Union he might not recognize were he alive today. In 2000 the U.S. population hovered just below three hundred million, with less than two percent of Americans employed in agriculture. Fifteen Amendments have been added to the Constitution Lincoln defended so unfailingly, and in 2008 a momentous event took place—one Lincoln himself could not have imagined—when the American people elected the first African-American president.

In a world that constantly seems to change at the speed of email, a nation looking for answers must be cautious about taking the past out of context or aggrandizing a national figure. It is far too easy to romanticize history—and to judge its participants— through the rosy lens of hindsight. But for all the differences between the nineteenth century and the twenty-first, the leadership skills developed and honed by Abraham Lincoln are timeless.

As a working man, Lincoln developed simple yet practical skills for dealing with the pressures of a heavy workload and balancing home-life with professional burdens. As a politician, he mastered the art of mass communication and compromise. As a leader, Lincoln envisioned a goal and attained it by tempering responsibility and determination with compassion and hope.

While no book will every truly allow us to re-create Abraham Lincoln's wisdom, or find out how he would deal with today's pressing problems, we believe he did leave behind an eternal legacy of leadership. Though the details differ, Americans in every socio-economic stratum face almost the same questions today as Lincoln did one hundred and fifty years ago: how to find equilibrium between work and life, how to interact personally and professionally, and how to meet the challenges that arise in a rapidly-evolving world.

For all the changes that took place during his lifetime, Lincoln fought for and succeeded in preserving a distinct democracy—one which does not try to forget, one which, for better or worse, folds the bloody lessons, painful memories, and awe-inspiring victories from the past into its present. For guidance in times of uncertainty and answers in an age of terrorism, housing bubbles, and health care crises, we can only turn to the scraps of paper left behind by a man who rose to the occasion when his nation called. Yet we believe that sometimes scraps of paper are enough to inspire a nation; and the test of a true leader can be found in a man who continues to inspire a country long after his own voice has faded to the echoes of time.

CHAPTER 1

TO LABOR WITH PURPOSE AND SUCCEED WITH DISCIPLINE

*"Leave nothing for tomorrow
which can be done today."*

A man, nameless to the annals of history except for a random chance of geographic proximity, once dared to look beyond the veil of martyred hindsight to remember a lanky yet surprisingly strong young man from Kentucky, "Abe Lincoln worked for me . . . didn't love work half as much as his pay. He said to me one day that his father taught him to work, but he never taught him to love it."

This charmingly unsentimental anecdote fits with what little is known about Lincoln's early years. Other neighbors interviewed years after Lincoln's death would recall watching Abe helping his father on the farm. The tall youth was known to faithfully, if not quite enthusiastically, perform the backbreaking labor required to survive on the frontiers of Kentucky, Indiana, and eventually Illinois.

No one would say Lincoln ever shied away from hard work; instead he saw physical labor as a means to an end. In his youth, that end was most often the chance stick his nose back in a book. As Lincoln grew in both wisdom and age, that end would become a defining and unshakable principle: the Union must be saved.

Lincoln's personal experiences as a "hired hand," lawyer, and eventually a politician, allowed him to develop a unique perspective on the American struggle to earn a living. For all the promise of opportunities and hope of the New World, few individuals in nineteenth-century America were truly able to rise above the standard of living they were born into. Even fewer were able to successfully navigate through both the spheres of physical laborer and intellectual professional. Though Lincoln undoubtedly enjoyed his career as a politician more than his life on the frontier, it can be argued he was definitely successful in both arenas.

The future president earned his first dollar ferrying passengers across the Ohio River on a raft he built himself. In the years that followed he worked his way up from hired hand to store clerk for one Mr. Denton Offutt. Eventually Lincoln was known as one of the most popular lawyers to travel the Illinois circuit court; whether he won or lost a case, he could always be counted on to tell a captivating yarn to the other legal professionals gathered around the inn hearth at night. Most obviously, as a politician, Lincoln attained the highest and most powerful civilian office in the country.

Impossible as it is to try and isolate one root cause for Lincoln's success, several themes do become obvious in his words below. Whether affixing his signature to a new law, swinging an axe above his head, or passionately calling a nation to arms, Lincoln was a man who diligently persevered. When there was a task to finish, he followed through; when there was a case to be won, he argued with passionate honesty; when there was a nation to save, he bore down with grit and determination.

Diligent Habits

Nothing valuable can be lost by taking time. If there be an object to hurry any of you in hot haste to a step which you would never take deliberately, that object will be frustrated by taking time; but no good object can be frustrated by it.

—Lincoln's First Inaugural Address;
March 4, 1861

You are not lazy, and still you are an idler. I doubt whether, since I saw you, you have done a good whole day's work in any one day. You do not very much dislike to work, and still you do not work much, merely because it does not seem to you that you could get much for it. This habit of uselessly wasting time is the whole difficulty; it is vastly important to you, and still more so to your children, that you should break the habit. It is more important to them, because they have longer to live, and can keep out of an idle habit before they are in it, easier than they can get out after they are in.

—Letter to J. D. Johnston; January 2, 1851

Some poet has said "Fools rush in where angels fear to tread." At the hazard of being thought one of the fools of this quotation, I meet that argument, I rush in, I take that bull by the horns.

—Reply to Stephen Douglas; October 16, 1854

If you intend to go to work, there is no better place than right where you are; if you do not intend to go to work you cannot get along anywhere. Squirming and crawling about from place to place can do no good.

—Letter J. D. Johnston; November 4, 1851

There may be some inequalities in the practical application of our system . . . .There may be mistakes made sometimes; and things may be done wrong, while the officers of the Government do all they can to prevent mistakes. But I beg of you, as citizens of this great Republic, not to let your minds be carried off from the great work we have before us. This struggle is too large for you to be diverted from it by any small matter.

—Address to the 164th Ohio Regiment; August 18, 1864

The advice of a father to his son "Beware of entrance to a quarrel, but being in, bear it that the opposed may beware thee" is good, and yet not best. Quarrel not at all. No man resolved to make the most of himself can spare time for personal contention. Still less can he afford to take all the consequences, including the vitiating of his temper, and the loss of self-control.

—Letter to Capt. James M. Cutts;
October 26, 1863

Cultivating a Successful Work Ethic and Mentality

Important principles may and must be inflexible.

—Lincoln's last public address;
April 11, 1865

Happy day, when, all appetites controlled, all poisons subdued, all matter subjected, mind, all conquering mind, shall live and move the monarch of the world. Glorious consummation! Hail fall of Fury! Reign of Reason, all hail!

—Address to the Washington Temperance Society;
February 22, 1842

Always bear in mind that your own resolution to succeed, is more important than any other one thing.

—Letter to Isham Reavis; November 5, 1855

Of course I would have preferred success; but failing in that, I have no regrets for having rejected all advice to the contrary, and resolutely made the struggle.

—Letter to Judge S. P. Chase; April 30, 1859

There may sometimes be ungenerous attempts to keep a young man down; and they will succeed, too, if he allows his mind to be diverted from its true channel to brood over the attempted injury.

—Letter to W. H. Herndon; July 10, 1848

All creation is a mine, and every man, a miner. The whole earth, and all within it, upon it, and round about it, including himself, in his physical, moral, and intellectual nature, and his susceptibilities, are the infinitely various "leads" from which, man, from the first, was to dig out his destiny.

—Lecture on Discoveries and Inventions; April 6, 1858

Now, as to the young men. You must not wait to be brought forward by the older men.

—Letter to W. H. Herndon; June 22, 1848

Determination and Self–Control

You can not fail in any laudable object, unless you allow your mind to be improperly directed.

—Letter to W. H. Herndon; July 10, 1848

But yet it is folly to undertake works of this or any kind, without first knowing that we are able to finish them, as half-finished work generally proves to be labor lost.

—Open letter to the People of Sangamo County; March 9, 1832

Every man is proud of what he does well; and no man is proud of what he does not do well. With the former, his heart is in his work; and he will do twice as much of it with less fatigue. The latter performs a little imperfectly, looks at it in disgust, turns from it, and imagines himself exceedingly tired. The little he has done, comes to nothing, for want of finishing.

—Address to the Wisconsin State Fair; September 30, 1859

Work, work, work, is the main thing.

—Letter to John M. Brockman; September 25, 1860

If anyone, upon his rare powers of speaking, shall claim an exemption from the drudgery of the law, his case is a failure in advance.

—Fragment; written circa July 1850

Will springs from the two elements of moral sense and self-interest.

—Speech given in reaction to the
Dred Scott decision; June 26, 1857

It behooves you to be wide awake and actively working.

—Letter to Joseph Gillespie;
July 16, 1858

Advancement—improvement in condition—is the order of things in a society of equals. As labor is the common burden of our race, so the effort of some to shift their share of the burden on to the shoulders of others is the great durable curse of the race.

—Fragment; written circa July 1854

You have confidence in yourself, which is a valuable, if not an indispensable quality. You are ambitious, which, within reasonable bounds, does good rather than harm.

—Letter to Maj. Gen. Hooker;
January 26, 1863

Towering genius disdains a beaten path. It seeks regions hitherto unexplored.

—Speech to the Young Men's Lyceum;
January 27, 1838

Work and Labor

I am always for the man who wishes to work.

—Endorsement for employment application;
August 15, 1864

Labor is the great source from which nearly all, if not all, human comforts and necessities are drawn.

—Speech at Cincinnati, Ohio;
September 17, 1859

The world is agreed that labor is the source from which human wants are mainly supplied. There is no dispute upon this point. From this point, however, men immediately diverge.

—Address at the Wisconsin State Fair;
September 30, 1859

The old general rule was that educated people did not perform manual labor.... But now, especially in these free states, nearly all are educated—quite too nearly all, to leave the labor of the uneducated, in any wise adequate to the support of the whole. It follows from this that henceforth educated people must labor.

—Address at the Wisconsin State Fair;
September 30, 1859

The strongest bond of human sympathy, outside the family relation, should be one uniting all working people, of all nations, and tongues, and kindreds.

—Reply to New York Workingmen's Democratic
Republican Association; March 21, 1864

The prudent, penniless beginner in the world labors for wages a while, saves a surplus with which to buy tools or land for himself, then labors on his own account another while, and at length hires another new beginner to help him. This is the just and generous and prosperous system which opens the way to all, gives hope to all, and consequent energy and progress and improvement of condition to all.

—Message to Congress; December 3, 1861

Property is the fruit of labor ... property is desirable ... is a positive good in the world. That some should be rich shows that others may become rich, and hence is just encouragement to industry and enterprise. Let not him who is houseless pull down the house of another; but let him labor diligently and build one for himself, thus by example assuring that his own shall be safe from violence when built.

—Reply to New York Workingmen's Democratic Republican Association; March 21, 1864

Labor is prior to and independent of capital. Capital is only the fruit of labor, and could never have existed if labor had not first existed. Labor is the superior of capital, and deserves much the higher consideration.

—Message to Congress; December 3, 1861

Labor is like any other commodity in the market— increase the demand for it, and you increase the price for it.

—Message to Congress; December 1, 1862

When one starts poor, as most do in the race of life, free society is such that he knows he can better his condition; he knows that there is no fixed condition of labor, for his whole life.

—Speech at New Haven, Connecticut;
March 6, 1860

No men living are more worthy to be trusted than those who toil up from poverty, none less inclined to take or touch aught which they have not honestly earned.

—Message to Congress; December 3, 1861

This is a world of compensation; and he who would be no slave, must consent to have no slave.

—Letter to Henry L. Pierce, & Others;
April 6, 1859

I don't believe in a law to prevent a man from getting rich; it would do more harm than good. So while we do not propose any war upon capital, we do wish to allow the humblest man an equal chance to get rich with everybody else.

—Speech at New Haven, Connecticut;
March 6, 1860

The Labor of Learning

Thoughtful men must feel that the fate of civilization upon this continent is involved in the issue of our contest. Among the most satisfying proofs of this conviction is the hearty devotion everywhere exhibited by our schools and colleges to the national cause.

—Letter to John Maclean; December 27, 1864

In all this, book-learning is available. A capacity, and taste, for reading, gives access to whatever has already been discovered by others. It is the key, or one of the keys, to the already solved problems. And not only so. It gives a relish, and facility, for successfully pursuing the yet unsolved ones.

—Address at the Wisconsin State Fair;
September 30, 1859

Upon the subject of education, not presuming to dictate any plan or system respecting it, I can only say that I view it as the most important subject which we as a people can be engaged in.

—Open letter to the People of Sangamo County;
March 9, 1832

Let reverence for the laws, be breathed by every American mother, to the lisping babe, that prattles on her lap; let it be taught in schools, in seminaries, and in colleges; let it be written in Primers, spelling books, and in Almanacs; let it be preached from the pulpit, proclaimed in legislative halls, and enforced in courts of justice. And, in short, let it become the political religion of the nation; and let the old and the young, the rich and the poor, the grave and the gay, of all sexes and tongues, and colors and conditions, sacrifice unceasingly upon its altars.

—Speech to the Young Men's Lyceum; January 27, 1838

Mr. Clay's lack of a more perfect early education, however it may be regretted generally, teaches at least one profitable lesson; it teaches that in this country, one can scarcely be so poor, but that, if he will, he can acquire sufficient education to get through the world respectably.

—Eulogy for Henry Clay; July 6, 1852

Lincoln as a Working Man

In law it is good policy to never plead what you need not, lest you oblige yourself to prove what you can not.

—Letter to Usher F. Linder; February 20, 1848

I find quite as much material for a lecture in those points wherein I have failed, as in those wherein I have been moderately successful. The leading rule for the lawyer, as for the man of every other calling, is diligence. Leave nothing for tomorrow which can be done today. Never let your correspondence fall behind. Whatever piece of business you have in hand, before stopping, do all the labor pertaining to it which can then be done.

—Fragment; written circa July 1850

If you wish to be a lawyer, attach no consequence to the place you are in, or the person you are with; but get books, sit down anywhere, and go to reading for yourself. That will make a lawyer of you quicker than any other way.

—Letter to William H. Grigsby; August 3, 1858

Let no man choosing the law for a calling for a moment yield to the popular belief—resolve to be honest at all events; and if in your own judgment you cannot be an honest lawyer, resolve to be honest without being a lawyer.

—Fragment; written circa July 1850

CHAPTER 2

THE MASTERY
AND ART OF
COMMUNICATION

"Public sentiment is everything."

Deep within the dark and dusty shelves of the Library of Congress lie two of the rarest photographs in American history. The first, bent and burnt with crisp edges crinkling on the sides, is a panoramic image of a crowd milling about on a grassy field and under a gray clouded sky. The second, similar in content to the first, is unique in that a tall stone gateway can be seen in the far distance at the left, while a perfectly erected canvas tent sits just at the right edge of the frame.

For all the scratches and distortions, each image conveys a sense of weighty anticipation. Civilians in stovetop hats and split coats are frozen mid-stride, their faces pointed resolutely toward some unknown destination. Intermixed in the crowd, Union soldiers in full uniform stand casually with their arms resting on their rifles, each poised and ready to be called to attention at a moment's notice.

Perhaps the most prominent feature of each photograph is the fact that almost every face in both images is utterly indistinguishable—thousands of individual features all blurred and condemned to obscurity by a technology unable to capture movement.

Yet this small historical defect is oddly appropriate, for these photographs were taken on November 19, 1863 at the dedication of the Union cemetery just outside of Gettysburg, Pennsylvania—the day President Abraham Lincoln delivered what is arguably the greatest speech in American history. This day was not meant to be preserved in images or photographs. Instead, it was a day forever enshrined in the American consciousness by words and words alone.

Almost as revered in history as the actual three-day battle itself, the Gettysburg Address is one of the most well-known pieces of writing in the American lexicon. On the day Lincoln actually gave his short speech, reviews were varied. Some called the speech "dull and commonplace" while others described hearing "a perfect gem." Whether witnesses appreciated or dismissed Lincoln's words, it is impossible to dismiss the weight of this singular piece of writing.

But why is the Gettysburg Address taught to generations of Americans almost one hundred and fifty years after it was delivered? What is it about those 278 simple words that allows them to echo in the American consciousness even today?

In part, the answer is because the Gettysburg Address is the essence of communication—the ability to create a message, an idea in other human beings, which lasts beyond lifetimes.

Lincoln's unparalleled ability to communicate, even from beyond the grave, can be traced to a combination of oratory skills, perceptiveness, and natural talent. As a lawyer, Lincoln learned to respect the power of persuasion—his living dependent on his ability to convince judges and peers that his opinion was correct. His experiences on the bench and on the campaign trail allowed him to hone verbal manipulation as well as master a few tricks of the trade. Perhaps most importantly, Lincoln appreciated the gravity of words, the weight of responsibility to live and act, not just preach. Edward Everett, the famed orator and keynote speaker at the Gettysburg dedication, captured Lincoln's communication skills best when he penned a note to the then-president the day after the ceremony, "I should be glad if I could flatter myself that I came as near to the central idea of the occasion in two hours as you did in two minutes."

The Power of the Public

In times like the present, men should utter nothing for which they would not willingly be responsible through time and in eternity.

—Message to Congress; December 1, 1862

Our government rests in public opinion. Whoever can change public opinion, can change the government, practically just so much. Public opinion, on any subject, always has a "central idea," from which all its minor thoughts radiate.

—Speech at the Republican banquet in Chicago; December 10, 1856

In this and like communities, public sentiment is everything. With public sentiment, nothing can fail; without it nothing can succeed. Consequently he who moulds public sentiment, goes deeper than he who enacts statutes or pronounces decisions.

—Reply to Stephen Douglas; August 21, 1858

You can fool all the people some of the time, and some of the people all the time, but you can not fool all the people all of the time.

—Fragment; written circa
May 1856

No party can command respect which sustains this year, what it opposed last.

—Letter to Judge Samuel Galloway;
July 28, 1859

The ballot is stronger than the bullet.

—Fragment; written circa
May 1856

Manipulating Definitions

The world has never had a good definition of the word "liberty," and the American people, just now, are much in want of one. We all declare for liberty; but in using the same word, we do not all mean the same thing.

—Address to the Sanitary Fair in Baltimore;
April 18, 1864

On the question of liberty, as a principle, we are not what we have been. When we were the political slaves of King George, and wanted to be free, we called the maxim that "all men are created equal" a self evident truth; but now when we have grown fat, and have lost all dread of being slaves ourselves, we have become so greedy to be masters that we call the same maxim "a self evident lie."

—Letter to George Robertson; August 15, 1855

It might seem at first thought to be of little difference whether the present movement at the South be called secession or rebellion. The movers, however, well understand the difference. At the beginning they knew they could never raise their treason to any respectable magnitude by any name which implies violation of law. . . . Accordingly, they commenced by an insidious debauching of the public mind. They invented an ingenious sophism which, if conceded, was followed by perfectly logical steps, through all the incidents, to the complete destruction of the Union. The sophism itself is that any State of the Union may consistently with the national Constitution, and therefore lawfully and peacefully, withdraw from the Union without the consent of the Union or of any other State. The little disguise that the supposed right is to be exercised only for just cause, themselves to be the sole judges of its justice, is too thin to merit any notice. With rebellion thus sugar-coated they have been drugging the public mind of their section for more than thirty years, and until at length they have brought many good men to a willingness to take up arms against the government the day after some assemblage of men have enacted the farcical pretence of taking their State out of the Union, who could have been brought to no such thing the day before.

—Message to Congress; July 4, 1861

The shepherd drives the wolf from the sheep's throat, for which the sheep thanks the shepherd as a liberator, while the wolf denounces him for the same act as the destroyer of liberty, especially as the sheep was a black one. Plainly the sheep and the wolf are not agreed upon a definition of the word liberty; and precisely the same difference prevails today among us human creatures, even in the North, and all professing to love liberty. Hence we behold the processes by which thousands are daily passing from under the yoke of bondage, hailed by some as the advance of liberty, and bewailed by others as the destruction of all liberty.

—Address to the Sanitary Fair in Baltimore; April 18, 1864

If any man at this day sincerely believes that the proper division of local from Federal authority . . . forbids the Federal Government to control as to slavery in the Federal Territories, he is right to say so, and to enforce his position by all truthful evidence and fair argument he can. But he has no right to mislead others who have less access to history, and less leisure to study it, into the false belief that "our fathers who framed the government under which we live" were of the same opinion—thus substituting falsehood and deception for truthful evidence and fair argument.

—Address at Cooper Institute; February 27, 1860

The words "coercion" and "invasion" are in great use about these days. Suppose we were simply to try if we can, and ascertain what is the meaning of these words. Let us get, if we can, the exact definition of these words—not from dictionaries, but from the men who constantly repeat them—what things they mean to express by the words. What, then, is "coercion"? What is "invasion"? Would the marching of an army into South Carolina, for instance, without the consent of her people, and in hostility against them, be coercion or invasion? I very frankly say, I think it would be invasion, and it would be coercion too, if the people of that country were forced to submit. But if the government, for instance, but simply insists upon holding its own forts, or retaking those forts which belong to it, or the enforcement of the laws of the United States in the collection of duties upon foreign importations, or even the withdrawal of the mails from those portions of the country where the mails themselves are habitually violated; would any or all of these things be coercion?

—Speech from the balcony of the Bates House in Indianapolis; February 11, 1861

If they had only pledged their judicial opinion that such right is affirmed in the instrument by implication, it would be open to others to show that neither the word "slave" nor "slavery" is to be found in the Constitution, nor the word "property" even, in any connection with language alluding to the things slave, or slavery, and that wherever in that instrument the slave is alluded to, he is called a "person;"—and wherever his master's legal right in relation to him is alluded to, it is spoken of as "service or labor which may be due,"—as a debt payable in service or labor. Also, it would be open to show, by contemporaneous history, that this mode of alluding to slaves and slavery, instead of speaking of them, was employed on purpose to exclude from the Constitution the idea that there could be property in man. To show all this, is easy and certain. When this obvious mistake of the Judges shall be brought to their notice, is it not reasonable to expect that they will withdraw the mistaken statement, and reconsider the conclusion based upon it?

—Address at Cooper Institute; February 27, 1860

I should like to know, taking this old Declaration of Independence, which declares that all men are equal upon principle, and making exceptions to it, where will it stop? If one man says it does not mean a Negro, why not another say it does not mean some other man?

—Reply to Stephen Douglas; July 10, 1858

Those Who Would Speak Must Bear Responsibilities

Neither let us be slandered from our duty by false accusations against us, nor frightened from it by menaces of destruction to the government nor of dungeons to ourselves.

—Address at Cooper Institute; February 27, 1860

I appeal to you again to constantly bear in mind that with you, and not with politicians, not with Presidents, not with office—seekers, but with you, is the question, "Shall the Union and shall the liberties of this country be preserved to the latest generation?"

—Speech at Indianapolis; February 11, 1861

It becomes my duty to make known to you—the people whom I propose to represent—my sentiments with regard to local affairs.

—Open letter to the People of Sangamo County; March 9, 1832

I may, therefore, have said something indiscreet, but I have said nothing but what I am willing to live by, and, in the pleasure of Almighty God, die by.

—Speech at Independence Hall; February 22, 1861

Fellow-citizens, I am not asserting anything; I am merely asking questions for you to consider.

—Speech at Indianapolis; February 12, 1861

It is with some hesitation I presume to address this letter and yet I wish not only you, but the whole Cabinet, and the President too, would consider the subject matter of it. My being among the people while you and they are not, will excuse the apparent presumption. It is understood that the President at first adopted, as a general rule, to throw the responsibility of the appointments upon the respective Departments; and that such rule is adhered to and practiced upon. This course I at first thought proper; and, of course, I am not now complaining of it. Still I am disappointed with the effect of it upon the public mind. It is fixing for the President the unjust and ruinous character of being a mere man of straw. This must be arrested, or it will damn us all inevitably. . . . The appointments need be no better than they have been, but the public must be brought to understand that they are the President's appointments. He must occasionally say, or seem to say, "by the Eternal," "I take the responsibility." Those phrases were the "Samson's locks" of Gen. Jackson, and we dare not disregard the lessons of experience.

—Letter to John M. Clayton; July 28, 1849

We know that there is not a perfect agreement of sentiment here on the public questions which might be rightfully considered in this convention, and that the indignation which we all must feel cannot be helped; but all of us must give up something for the good of the cause.

—Speech; May 29, 1856

I believe it is an established maxim in morals that he who makes an assertion without knowing whether it is true or false, is guilty of falsehood; and the accidental truth of the assertion, does not justify or excuse him.

—Letter to Allen N. Ford; August 11, 1846

Tips for a Worthy Wordsmith

When the conduct of men is designed to be influenced, persuasion, kind, unassuming persuasion, should ever be adopted. It is an old and a true maxim, that a "drop of honey catches more flies than a gallon of gall."

—Speech to the Washington Temperance Society; February 22, 1842

Everyone likes a compliment.

—Letter to Thurlow Weed; March 15, 1865

When a man bears himself somewhat misrepresented, it provokes him—at least, I find it so with myself; but when misrepresentation becomes very gross and palpable, it is more apt to amuse him.

—Reply to Stephen Douglas; August 21, 1858

If you would win a man to your cause, first convince him that you are his sincere friend. Therein is a drop of honey that catches his heart, which, say what he will, is the great highroad to his reason, and which, when once gained, you will find but little trouble in convincing his judgment of the justice of your cause, if indeed that cause really be a just one. On the contrary, assume to dictate to his judgment, or to command his action, or to mark him as one to be shunned and despised, and he will retreat within himself, close all the avenues to his head and his heart; and tho' your cause be naked truth itself, transformed to the heaviest lance, harder than steel, and sharper than steel can be made, and tho' you throw it with more than Herculean force and precision, you shall no more be able to pierce him, than to penetrate the hard shell of a tortoise with a rye straw. Such is man, and so must he be understood by those who would lead him, even to his own best interest.

—Speech to the Washington Temperance Society;
February 22, 1842

Men are not flattered by being shown that there has been a difference of purpose between the Almighty and them.

—Letter to Thurlow Weed; March 15, 1865

Human action can be modified to some extent, but human nature cannot be changed.

—Address at Cooper Institute; February 27, 1860

But, fellow-citizens, I shall conclude . . . upon the subjects of which I have treated, I have spoken as I thought. I may be wrong in regard to any or all of them; but holding it a sound maxim, that it is better to be only sometimes right, than at all times wrong, so soon as I discover my opinions to be erroneous, I shall be ready to renounce them.

—Open letter to the People of Sangamo County; March 9, 1832

I have endured a great deal of ridicule without much malice; and have received a great deal of kindness, not quite free from ridicule. I am used to it.

—Letter to James H. Hackett; November 2, 1863

I never encourage deceit, and falsehood, especially if you have got a bad memory, is the worst enemy a fellow can have. The fact is truth is your truest friend, no matter what the circumstances are. Notwithstanding this copy-book preamble, my boy, I am inclined to suggest a little prudence on your part.

—Letter to George E. Pickett; February 22, 1842

I do not feel justified to enter upon the broad field you present in regard to the political differences between radicals and conservatives. From time to time I have done and said what appeared to me proper to do and say. The public knows it all. It obliges nobody to follow me. The radicals and conservatives, each agree with me in some things, and disagree in others. I could wish both to agree with me in all things; for then they would agree with each other, and would be too strong for any foe from any quarter. They, however, choose to do otherwise, and I do not question their right. I too shall do what seems to be my duty.

—Letter to Charles D. Drake & Others;
October 5, 1863

Invoking the Earnest Emotions Behind the Words

That is the issue that will continue in this country when these poor tongues of Judge Douglas and myself shall be silent. It is the eternal struggle between these two principles—right and wrong—throughout the world. They are the two principles that have stood face to face from the beginning of time, and will ever continue to struggle. The one is the common right of humanity and the other the divine right of kings.

—Reply to Stephen Douglas; October 15, 1858

In a great national crisis like ours unanimity of action among those seeking a common end is very desirable—almost indispensable. And yet no approach to such unanimity is attainable unless some deference shall be paid to the will of the majority simply because it is the will of the majority.

—Message to Congress; December 6, 1864

A house divided against itself cannot stand. I believe this government cannot endure permanently half slave and half free. I do not expect the Union to be dissolved—I do not expect the house to fall—but I do expect it will cease to be divided. It will become all one thing, or all the other.

—Speech accepting the Republican nomination for Senate; June 16, 1858

Our reliance is in the love of liberty which God has planted in our bosoms. Our defense is in the preservation of the spirit which prizes liberty as the heritage of all men, in all lands, everywhere.

—Speech at Edwardsville, Illinois; September 11, 1858

The Art of Rhetoric

Ladies and Gentlemen, I have no speech to make to you, and no time to speak in. I appear before you that I may see you, and that you may see me; and I am willing to admit, that, so far as the ladies are concerned, I have the best of the bargain, though I wish it to be understood that I do not make the same acknowledgment concerning the men.

—Address at Utica, New York;
February 18, 1861

I am not accustomed to the language of eulogy. I have never studied the art of paying compliments to women. But I must say, that if all that has been said by orators and poets since the creation of the world in praise of women were applied to the women of America, it would not do them justice for their conduct during this war. I will close by saying, God bless the women of America!

—Address to the Sanitary Fair in Washington D.C.;
March 18, 1864

I have always thought that all men should be free; but if any should be slaves, it should be first those who desire it for themselves, and secondly those who desire it for others. Whenever I hear any one arguing for slavery I feel a strong impulse to see it tried on him personally.

> —Address to the 140th Indiana Regiment;
> March 17, 1865

I leave you, hoping that the lamp of liberty will burn in your bosoms until there shall no longer be a doubt that all men are created free and equal.

> —Reply to Stephen Douglas; July 10, 1858

I am rather inclined to silence, and whether that be wise or not, it is at least more unusual nowadays to find a man who can hold his tongue than to find one who cannot.

> —Address at Monogahela House in Pittsburgh;
> February 14, 1861

Extemporaneous speaking should be practiced and cultivated. It is the lawyer's avenue to the public. However able and faithful he may be in other respects, people are slow to bring him business if he cannot make a speech. And yet there is not a more fatal error to young lawyers than relying too much on speech-making.

> —Fragment; written circa July 1850

Fellow–citizens, I am very greatly rejoiced to find that an occasion has occurred so pleasurable that the people cannot restrain themselves. . . . I see you have a band of music with you. I propose closing up this interview by the band performing a particular tune which I will name. Before it is done, however, I wish to mention one or two little circumstances connected with it. I have always thought "Dixie" one of the best tunes I have ever heard. Our adversaries over the way attempted to appropriate it, but I insisted yesterday that we fairly captured it. I presented the question to the Attorney General, and he gave it as his legal opinion that it is our lawful prize.

—Lincoln's spontaneous address to a crowd that had gathered at the White House to celebrate news of General Lee's surrender; April 10, 1865

Navigating the Dangers of Public Opinion

And now a word of caution. Our adversaries think they can gain a point if they could force me to openly deny the charge, by which some degree of offence would be given to the Americans. For this reason it must not publicly appear that I am paying any attention to the charge.[1]

—Letter to A. Jonas; July 21, 1860

---

[1] The "charge" referred to states that Lincoln spent a night at a lodge run by supporters of the Know–Nothing Party.

Every word is so closely noted that it will not do to make trivial ones.

—Speech at Frederick, Maryland;
October 4, 1862

We live in the midst of alarms; anxiety beclouds the future; we expect some new disaster with each newspaper we read. Are we in a healthful political state? Are not the tendencies plain? Do not the signs of the times point plainly the way in which we are going?

—Speech at Bloomington, Illinois;
May 29, 1856

DEAR SIR:—Your letter enclosing the attack of the *Times* upon me was received this morning. Give yourself no concern about my voting against the supplies. Unless you are without faith that a lie can be successfully contradicted, there is not a word of truth in the charge, and I am just considering a little as to the best shape to put a contradiction in. Show this to whomever you please, but do not publish it in the paper.

—Letter to H. C. Whitney; June 24, 1858

As a general rule I abstain from reading the reports of attacks upon myself, wishing not to be provoked by that to which I cannot properly offer an answer.

—Lincoln's last public address; April 11, 1865

Understanding the Opposing Mindset

Let us understand this. I am not, just here, trying to prove that we are right and they are wrong. I have been stating where we and they stand, and trying to show what is the real difference between us.

—Reply to Stephen Douglas; October 13, 1858

The will of God prevails. In great contests each party claims to act in accordance with the will of God. Both may be, and one must be, wrong.

—Meditation on Divine Will; written circa September 1862

I admit that slavery is at the root of the rebellion, or at least its sine qua non. The ambition of politicians may have instigated them to act, but they would have been impotent without slavery as their instrument. I will also concede that emancipation would help us in Europe, and convince them that we are incited by something more than ambition. I grant further, that it would help somewhat at the North, though not so much, I fear, as you and those you represent, imagine. . . . I will mention another thing, though it meet only your scorn and contempt. There are fifty thousand bayonets in the Union armies from the border slave States. It would be a serious matter if, in consequence of a proclamation such as you desire, they should go over to the rebels. I do not think they all would,—not so many indeed, as a year ago, nor as six months ago; not so many to-day as yesterday. Every day increases their Union feeling. They are also getting their pride enlisted, and want to beat the rebels. Let me say one thing more: I think you should admit that we already have an important principle to rally and unite the people, in the fact that constitutional government is at stake. This is a fundamental idea, going down about as deep as anything. Do not misunderstand me because I have mentioned these objections. They indicate the difficulties that have thus far prevented my action in some such way as you desire. I have not decided against a proclamation of liberty to the slaves, but hold the matter under advisement. And I can assure you that the subject is on my mind by day and night, more than any other. Whatever shall appear to be God's will, I will do. I trust that in the freedom with which I have canvassed your views, I have not in any respect injured your feelings.

—Reply to the Chicago Committee of United Religious Denominations; September 13, 1862

What is true, however, of him who heads the insurgent cause is not necessarily true of those who follow.

—Message to Congress; December 6, 1864

The slaveholder does not like to be considered a mean fellow for holding that species of property, and hence, he has to struggle within himself and sets about arguing himself into the belief that slavery is right. The property influences his mind. . . . Whether the owners of this species of property do really see it as it is, it is not for me to say, but if they do, they see it as it is through two thousand millions of dollars, and that is a pretty thick coating. Certain it is that they do not see it as we see it. Certain it is that this two thousand millions of dollars, invested in this species of property, all so concentrated that the mind can grasp it at once—this immense pecuniary interest— has its influence upon their minds.

—Speech at New Haven, Connecticut; March 6, 1860

You cannot destroy that judgment and feeling—that sentiment—by breaking up the political organization which rallies around it. You can scarcely scatter and disperse an army which has been formed into order in the face of your heaviest fire; but if you could, how much would you gain by forcing the sentiment which created it out of the peaceful channel of the ballot-box, into some other channel?

—Address at Cooper Institute; February 27, 1860

If the loyal people, united, were put to the utmost of their strength by the rebellion, must they not fail when divided, and partially paralyzed, by a political war among themselves?

—Speech at the White House; November 10, 1864

No one man has authority to give up the rebellion for any other man.

—Lincoln's last public address; April 11, 1865

Thinking it right, as they do, they are not to blame for desiring its full recognition, as being right; but, thinking it wrong, as we do, can we yield to them?

—Address at Cooper Institute; February 27, 1860

The ant, who has toiled and dragged a crumb to his nest, will furiously defend the fruit of his labor, against whatever robber assails him. So plain, that the most dumb and stupid slave that ever toiled for a master, does constantly know that he is wronged. So plain that no one, high or low, ever does mistake it, except in a plainly selfish way; for although volume upon volume is written to prove slavery is a very good thing, we never hear of the man who wishes to take the good of it, by being a slave himself.

—Fragment; written circa July 1854

Four score and seven years ago, our fathers brought forth upon this continent a new nation: conceived in liberty, and dedicated to the proposition that all men are created equal. Now we are engaged in a great civil war testing whether that nation, or any nation so conceived and so dedicated can long endure. We are met on a great battlefield of that war. We have come to dedicate a portion of that field as a final resting place for those who here gave their lives that this nation might live. It is altogether fitting and proper that we should do this. But, in a larger sense, we cannot dedicate, we cannot consecrate, we cannot hallow this ground. The brave men, living and dead, who struggled here have consecrated it, far above our poor power to add or detract. The world will little note, nor long remember, what we say here, but it can never forget what they did here. It is for us the living, rather, to be dedicated here to the unfinished work which they who fought here have thus far so nobly advanced. It is rather for us to be here dedicated to the great task remaining before us, that from these honored dead we take increased devotion to that cause for which they gave the last full measure of devotion, that we here highly resolve that these dead shall not have died in vain, that this nation, under God, shall have a new birth of freedom, and that government of the people, by the people, for the people, shall not perish from this earth.

—Gettysburg Address; November 19, 1863

CHAPTER 3

RESPONSIBILITIES
AND BURDENS OF
LEADERSHIP

"Fellow citizens, we cannot escape history."

One month before Abraham Lincoln took the oath of office, the Texas State Legislature issued the *Joint Resolution Relative to Coercion.* This short and bold document captured the unapologetic pride that ran rampant among many Southern politicians just before the start of the Civil War. More importantly, it identified one of the most potent fears among white Southerners—a fear so strong that it helped fill the ranks of the Confederate Army for almost four years, "we shall make common cause . . . in resisting by all means and to the last extremity such unconstitutional violence and tyrannical usurpation of power."

Historians will debate the causes and triggers of the Civil War for generations to come, but undeniably, at the root of at least some of the bloodshed lies the question of power. Which body is legally supreme, the Federal or State government? Who has the stronger army and navy? Does one man have the right to own another? Does one region have the right to impose its values over another?

Perhaps the bloodiest laboratory in American history, the Civil War was essentially an experimentation in power. The questions left unanswered by the Founding Fathers were explored on gore-filled battlefields and examined under the bloody lens of trial and error.

Yet despite the chaos and rending of the governmental fabric, the purpose of power could not have been demonstrated more profoundly than by Abraham Lincoln. At a time when all the precedents that had come before were washed away, President Lincoln forged a unique balance between unyielding determination and flexibility. He admitted when he was wrong, found new ways to adapt to challenges, and most importantly, he never stopped questioning the source of his own power.

Perhaps the greatest testament to Lincoln's leadership skills is the fact that he defined his role in the conflict to be that of public servant. His actions, positive and negative, could all be traced back his oath of office. Lincoln swore to uphold the Constitution and was willing to do everything necessary—even if it disagreed with his own personal philosophy—to fulfill the vow he took on the day he became president.

There is a tragic irony in reading passionate words of freedom when they were proclaimed by Southern men who sought to own others. But when read in contrast to Lincoln's own words, they offer a profound lesson: power is merely a tool of man. What is tyranny to one person is the means to achieve freedom to another. True leaders are not those who simply wield power, they are the ones willing to question their own, and determine the purpose behind such might.

∞

The Power to Serve

Every man is said to have his peculiar ambition. Whether it be true or not, I can say, for one, that I have no other so great as that of being truly esteemed of my fellow-men, by rendering myself worthy of their esteem. How far I shall succeed in gratifying this ambition is yet to be developed.

—Open letter to the People of Sangamo County;
March 19, 1832

I freely acknowledge myself the servant of the people, according to the bond of service—the United States Constitution; and that, as such, I am responsible to them.

—Letter to James C. Conkling; August 26, 1863

I am filled with deep emotion at finding myself standing here, in this place, where were collected together the wisdom, the patriotism, the devotion to principle, from which sprang the institutions under which we live. You have kindly suggested to me that in my hands is the task of restoring peace to the present distracted condition of the country. I can say in return, Sir, that all the political sentiments I entertain have been drawn, so far as I have been able to draw them, from the sentiments which originated and were given to the world from this hall. I have never had a feeling politically that did not spring from the sentiments embodied in the Declaration of Independence.

—Speech at Independence Hall;
February 22, 1861

I fully appreciate the present peril the country is in, and the weight of responsibility on me.

—Letter to Alexander Stephens;
December 22, 1860

If there is anything wanting which is within my power to give, do not fail to let me know it.

—Letter to Gen. Grant;
April 30, 1864

If I could save the Union without freeing any slave, I would do it; if I could save it by freeing all the slaves, I would do it.

—Letter to Horace Greeley; August 22, 1862

Most governments have been based, practically, on the denial of equal rights of men, as I have, in part, stated them; ours began, by affirming those rights. They said, some men are too ignorant, and vicious to share in government. Possibly so, said we; and, by your system, you would always keep them ignorant, and vicious. We proposed to give all a chance; and we expected the weak to grow stronger, the ignorant, wiser; and all the better, and happier together. We made the experiment; and the fruit is before us. Look at it—think of it.

—Fragment; written circa July 1854

I recollect thinking then, boy even though I was, that there must have been something more than common that these men struggled for. I am exceedingly anxious that that thing, that something even more than national independence; that something that held out a great promise to all the people of the world for all time to come, I am exceedingly anxious that this Union, the Constitution, and the liberties of the people shall be perpetuated in accordance with the original idea for which the struggle was made, and I shall be most happy indeed if I shall be an humble instrument in the hands of the Almighty, and of this, His most chosen people, for perpetuating the object of that great struggle.

—Speech at Trenton, New Jersey;
February 21, 1861

I therefore consider that, in view of the Constitution and the laws, the Union is unbroken; and, to the extent of my ability, I shall take care, as the Constitution itself expressly enjoins upon me, that the laws of the Union be faithfully executed in all the states. Doing this I deem to be only a simple duty on my part; and I shall perform it, so far as practicable, unless my rightful masters, the American people, shall withhold the requisite means, or, in some authoritative manner, direct the contrary. I trust this will not be regarded as a menace, but only as the declared purpose of the Union that it will constitutionally defend, and maintain itself.

—Lincoln's first Inaugural Address;
March 4, 1861

Fellow-citizens, we cannot escape history. We of this Congress and this administration, will be remembered in spite of ourselves. No personal significances, or insignificance, can spare one or another of us. The fiery trial through which we pass, will light us down, in honor or dishonor, to the latest generation. We say we are for the Union. The world knows we do know how to save it.

—Message to Congress; December 1, 1862

The Purpose of Power

At what point then is the approach of danger to be expected? I answer, if it ever reach us, it must spring up amongst us. It cannot come from abroad. If destruction be our lot, we must ourselves be its author and finisher. As a nation of freemen, we must live through all time, or die by suicide.

—Speech to the Young Men's Lyceum;
January 27, 1838

We, even we here, hold the power and bear the responsibility. In giving freedom to the slave, we assure freedom to the free, honorable alike in what we give and what we preserve. We shall nobly save or meanly lose the last, best hope of earth.

—Message to Congress; December 1, 1862

When the white man governs himself that is self-government; but when he governs himself and also governs another man, that is more than self-government—that is despotism.

—Reply to Stephen Douglas; October 16, 1854

I do not mean to say that this general government is charged with the duty of redressing or preventing all the wrongs in the world; but I do think that it is charged with the duty of preventing and redressing all wrongs which are wrongs to itself.

—Speech at Cincinnati, Ohio;
September 17, 1859

As I would not be a slave, so I would not be a master. This expresses my idea of democracy. Whatever differs from this, to the extent of the difference, is no democracy.

—Fragment; written circa August 1858

What I do say is, that no man is good enough to govern another man, without that other's consent. I say this is the leading principle—the sheet anchor of American republicanism.

—Reply to Stephen Douglas; October 16, 1854

Those who deny freedom to others, deserve it not for themselves; and, under a just God, cannot long retain it.

—Letter to Henry L. Pierce, & Others;
April 6, 1859

Negroes, like other people, act upon motives. Why should they do anything for us, if we will do nothing for them? If they stake their lives for us, they must be prompted by the strongest motive, even the promise of freedom. And the promise being made, must be kept.

—Letter to James C. Conkling; August 26, 1863

Yet notwithstanding all this, if the laws be continually despised and disregarded, if their rights to be secure in their persons and property, are held by no better tenure than the caprice of a mob, the alienation of their affections from the government is the natural consequence; and to that, sooner or later, it must come. Here then, is one point at which danger may be expected. The question recurs "how shall we fortify against it?" The answer is simple. Let every American, every lover of liberty, every well-wisher to his posterity, swear by the blood of the Revolution, never to violate in the least particular, the laws of the country; and never to tolerate their violation by others. As the patriots of Seventy-six did to the support of the Declaration of Independence, so to

the support of the Constitution and laws, let every
American pledge his life, his property, and his sacred
honor; let every man remember that to violate the
law, is to trample on the blood of his father, and to
tear the charter of his own, and his children's liberty.

—Speech to the Young Men's Lyceum;
January 27, 1838

We have, as all will agree, a free Government, where
every man has a right to be equal with every other
man. In this great struggle, this form of Government
and every form of human right is endangered if our
enemies succeed.

—Address to the 164th Ohio Regiment;
August 18, 1864

The people . . . have thus allowed this giant insurrec-
tion to make its nest within her borders,—and this
government has no choice left but to deal with it
where it finds it. And it has the less regret, as the loyal
citizens have in due form claimed its protection.

—Message to Congress; July 4, 1861

It is not merely for today, but for all time to come that
we should perpetuate for our children's children this

great and free government, which we have enjoyed all
our lives.

> —Address to the 166th Regiment;
> August 22, 1864

Justified Power

The legitimate object of government, is to do for a
community of people, whatever they need to have
done, but cannot do, at all, or cannot, so well do,
for themselves—in their separate, and individual
capacities. In all that the people can individually
do as well for themselves, government ought not to
interfere.

> —Fragment; written circa July 1854

If we shall constitutionally elect a President, it
will be our duty to see that you submit. Old John
Brown has been executed for treason against a State.
We cannot object, even though he agreed with us
in thinking slavery wrong. That cannot excuse
violence, bloodshed and treason. It could avail him
nothing that he might think himself right. So, if we
constitutionally elect a President, and therefore you
undertake to destroy the Union, it will be our duty to
deal with you as old John Brown has been dealt with.

We shall try to do our duty. We hope and believe that in no section will a majority so act as to render such extreme measures necessary.

—Speech given at Levenworth, Kansas;
December 1859

Let us have faith that right makes might, and in that faith, let us, to the end, dare to do our duty as we understand it.

—Address at Cooper Institute; February 27, 1860

It is true, as has been said by the president of the Senate, that a very great responsibility rests upon me in the position to which the votes of the American people have called me. I am deeply sensible of that weighty responsibility. I cannot but know, what you all know, that without a name, perhaps without a reason why I should have a name, there has fallen upon me a task such as did not rest even upon the Father of his Country; and so feeling, I cannot but turn and look for that support without which it will be impossible for me to perform that great task. I turn then, and look to the great American people, and to that God who has never forsaken them.

—Speech to the State Legislature at
Columbus, Ohio; February 13, 1861

We cannot have free government without elections; and if the rebellion could force us to forego or postpone a national election, it might fairly claim to have already conquered and ruined us.

—Reply to a spontaneous serenade;
November 10, 1864

I am naturally anti-slavery. If slavery is not wrong, nothing is wrong. I cannot remember when I did not so think and feel, and yet I have never understood that the Presidency conferred upon me an unrestricted right to act officially upon this judgment and feeling. It was in the oath that I took, that I would, to the best of my ability, preserve, protect, and defend the Constitution of the United States. I could not take office without taking the oath. Nor was it my view that I might take an oath to get power, and break the oath in using the power.

—Letter to A. G. Hodges; April 4, 1984

When I came, on the 4th of March, 1861, through a free and constitutional election to fireside in the Government of the United States, the country was found at the verge of civil war. Whatever might have been the cause, or whosesoever the fault, one duty, paramount to all others, was before me, namely, to maintain and preserve at once the Constitution and the integrity of the Federal Republic. A conscientious purpose to perform this duty is the key to all the measures of administration which have been and to all which will hereafter be pursued. Under our frame of government and my official oath, I could not depart from this purpose if I would.

—Reply to the Working Men of
Manchester, England; January 1863

But the proclamation, as law, either is valid or is not valid. If it is not valid, it needs no retraction. If it is valid, it cannot be retracted any more than the dead can be brought to life.

—Letter to James C. Conkling; August 26, 1863

Leadership vs. Tyranny

If a state, in one instance, and a county in another, should be equal in extent of territory, and equal in the number of people, wherein is that state any better than the county? Can a change of name change the right?

—Speech at Indianapolis, Illinois;
February 11, 1861

If the minority will not acquiesce, that majority must, or the government must cease. There is no other alternative; for continuing the government, is acquiescence on one side or the other.

—Lincoln's first Inaugural Address; March 4, 1861

What mysterious right to play tyrant is conferred on a district of country, with its people, by merely calling it a State?

—Speech at Indianapolis, Illinois; February 12, 1861

Under these circumstances I have been urgently solicited to establish, by military power, courts to administer summary justice in such cases. I have thus far declined to do it, not because I had any doubt that the end proposed—the collection of the debts— was just and right in itself, but because I have been unwilling to go beyond the pressure of necessity in the unusual exercise of power.

—Message to Congress; December 3, 1861

The assertion that "all men are created equal" was of no practical use in effecting our separation from Great Britain; and it was placed in the Declaration, not for that, but for future use. Its authors meant it to be as, thank God, it is now proving itself, a stumbling block to those who in after times might seek to turn a free people back into the hateful paths of despotism.

> —Speech given in reaction to the
> Dred Scott decision; June 26, 1857

Boldly Pursue Your Goals

You desire peace, and you blame me that we do not have it. But how can we attain it?

> —Letter to James C. Conkling; August 26, 1863

As to the policy I "seem to be pursuing," as you say, I have not meant to leave any one in doubt. I would save the Union.

> —Letter to Horace Greeley; August 22, 1862

In stating a single condition of peace, I mean simply to say that the war will cease on the part of the government, whenever it shall have ceased on the part of those who began it.

> —Message to Congress; December 6, 1864

I am a patient man—always willing to forgive on the Christian terms of repentance; and also to give ample time for repentance. Still I must save this government if possible. What I cannot do, of course I will not do; but it may as well be understood, once and for all, that I shall not surrender this game leaving any available card unplayed.

—Letter to Reverdy Johnson; July 26, 1862

By general law, life and limb must be protected, yet often a limb must be amputated to save a life; but a life is never wisely given to save a limb. I felt that measures, otherwise unconstitutional, might become lawful by becoming indispensable to the preservation of the Constitution through the preservation of the nation. Right or wrong, I assumed this ground; and now avow it. I could not feel that, to the best of my ability, I had even tried to preserve the Constitution, if, to save slavery or any minor matter, I should permit the wreck of government, country, and Constitution, all together.

—Letter to A. G. Hodges; April 4, 1864

What would you do in my position? Would you drop the war where it is, or would you prosecute it in the future with elder—stalk squirts charged with rose-water? Would you deal lighter blows rather than heavier ones? Would you give up the contest, leaving any available means untried? I am in no boastful mood. I shall not do more than I can, and I shall do all I can to save the government, which is my sworn duty as well as my personal inclination.

—Letter to Cutherbert Bullitt; July 28, 1862

Much is being said about peace; and no man desires peace more ardently than I. Still I am yet unprepared to give up the Union for a peace which, so achieved, could not be of much duration.

—Letter to Isaac Schermerhorn;
September 12, 1864

I shall do less whenever I shall believe what I am doing hurts the cause, and I shall do more whenever I shall believe doing more will help the cause. I shall try to correct errors where shown to be errors, and I shall adopt new views as fast as they shall appear to be true views . . . I have here stated my views of official duty, and I intend no modification of my oft-expressed personal wish that all men everywhere could be free.

—Letter to Horace Greely; August 22, 1862

Let us be diverted by none of those sophistical contrivances wherewith we are so industriously plied and belabored—contrivances such as groping for some middle ground between the right and the wrong, vain as the search for a man who should be neither a living man nor a dead man—such as a policy of "don't care" on a question about which all true men do care.

—Address at Cooper Institute; February 27, 1860

Emotional Control

Passion has helped us; but can do so no more. It will in future be our enemy. Reason, cold, calculating, unimpassioned reason, must furnish all the material for our future support and defense. Let those materials be molded into general intelligence, sound morality and, in particular, a reverence for the Constitution and laws. . . . Upon these let the proud fabric of freedom rest, as the rock of its basis; and as truly as has been said of the only greater institution, "the gates of hell shall not prevail against it."

—Speech to the Young Men's Lyceum; January 27, 1838

I hope it will not be irreverent for me to say, that if it is probable that God would reveal His will to others, on a point [emancipation of the slaves] so connected with my duty, it might be supposed that He would reveal it directly to me; for, unless I am more deceived in myself than I often am, it is my earnest desire to know the will of Providence in this matter. And if I can learn what it is, I will do it. These are not, however, the days of miracles, and I suppose it will be granted that I am not to expect a direct revelation. I must study the plain physical facts of the case, ascertain what is possible and learn what appears to be wise and right.

—Reply to the Chicago Committee of United Religious Denominations; September 13, 1862

The true role, in determining to embrace, or reject any thing, is not whether it have any evil in it; but whether it have more of evil, than of good. There are few things wholly evil, or wholly good. Almost everything, especially of governmental policy, is an inseparable compound of the two; so that our best judgment of the preponderance between them is continually demanded.

—Speech in the House of Representatives; June 20, 1848

We do not today know that a colored soldier, or white officer commanding colored soldiers, has been massacred by the rebels when made a prisoner. We fear it, we believe it, I may say,—but we do not know it. To take the life of one of their prisoners on the assumption that they murder ours, when it is short of certainty that they do murder ours, might be too serious, too cruel, a mistake. We are having the

Fort Pillow affair thoroughly investigated; and such investigation will probably show conclusively how the truth is. . . . If there has been the massacre of three hundred there, or even the tenth part of three hundred, it will be conclusively proved; and being so proved, the retribution shall as surely come. It will be matter of grave consideration in what exact course to apply the retribution; but in the supposed case it must come.

—Address to the Sanitary Fair in Baltimore;
April 18, 1864

It is my duty to hear all; but, at last, I must, within my sphere, judge what to do, and what to forbear.

—Letter to Charles D. Drake & Others;
October 5, 1863

I view this matter [emancipation of the slaves] as a practical war-measure, to be decided on according to the advantages or disadvantages it may offer to the suppression of the rebellion.

—Reply to the Chicago Committee of United
Religious Denominations; September 13, 1862

Flexibility to Adapt to New Challenges

The dogmas of the quiet past, are inadequate to the stormy present. The occasion is piled high with difficulty, and we must rise with the occasion. As our case is new, so we must think anew, and act anew. We must disenthrall ourselves, and then we shall save our country.

—Message to Congress; December 1, 1862

The principles of Jefferson are the definitions and axioms of free society. . . . All honor to Jefferson to the man who, in the concrete pressure of a struggle for national independence by a single people, had the coolness, forecast, and capacity to introduce into a mere revolutionary document an abstract truth, applicable to all men and all times, and so to embalm it there that to-day and in all coming days it shall be a rebuke and a stumbling-block to the very harbingers of reappearing tyranny and oppression.

—Letter to H. L. Pierce & Others; April 6, 1859

What I do about slavery, and the colored race, I do because I believe it helps to save the Union; and what I forbear, I forbear because I do not believe it would help to save the Union . . . I shall try to correct errors when shown to be errors; and I shall adopt new views so fast as they shall appear to be true views.

—Letter to Horace Greeley; August 22, 1862

Accountability and Criticism

He who does something at the head of one regiment, will eclipse him who does nothing at the head of a hundred.

—Letter to Maj. Gen. Hunter;
December 31, 1861

This government cannot much longer play a game in which it stakes all, and its enemies stake nothing. Those enemies must understand that they cannot experiment for ten years trying to destroy the government, and if they fail still come back into the Union unhurt.

—Letter to August Belmont; July 31, 1862

I have placed you at the head of the Army of the Potomac. Of course I have done this upon what appear to me to be sufficient reasons. And yet I think it best for you to know that there are some things in regard to which, I am not quite satisfied with you. I believe you to be a brave and skilful soldier, which, of course, I like. I also believe you do not mix politics with your profession, in which you are right. . . . But I think that during Gen. Burnside's command of the army, you have taken counsel of your ambition, and thwarted him as much as you could, in which you did a great wrong to the country, and to a most meritorious and honorable brother officer. I have heard, in such way as to believe it, of your recently saying that both the army and the government needed a dictator. Of course it was not for this, but in spite of it, that I have given you the command. Only those generals who gain successes, can set up dictators. What I now ask of you is military success, and I will risk the dictatorship. The government will support you to the utmost of its ability, which is neither more nor less than it has done and will do for all commanders. I much fear that the spirit which you have aided to infuse into the army, of criticizing their commander, and withholding confidence from him, will now turn upon you. I shall assist you as far as I can, to put it down. Neither you, nor Napoleon, if he were alive again, could get any good out of an army, while such a spirit prevails in it. And now, beware of rashness. Beware of rashness but with energy, and sleepless vigilance, go forward, and give us victories.

—Letter to Maj. Gen. Hooker;
January 26, 1863

It is not my purpose to review our discussions with foreign states, because, whatever might be their wishes or dispositions, the integrity of our country and the stability of our Government mainly depend not upon them, but on the loyalty, virtue, patriotism, and intelligence of the American people.

—Lincoln's first State of the Union Address;
December 3, 1861

I regret to find you denouncing so many persons as liars, scoundrels, fools, thieves, and persecutors of yourself. Your military position looks critical, but did anybody force you into it? Have you been ordered to confront and fight ten thousand men, with three thousand men? The government cannot make men; and it is very easy, when a man has been given the highest commission, for him to turn on those who gave it and vilify them for not giving him a command according to his rank.

—Letter to Maj. Gen. Blunt;
August 18, 1863

If, then, I was guilty of such conduct, I should blame no man who should condemn me for it; but I do blame those, whoever they may be who falsely put such a charge in circulation against me.

—Open letter to the Voters of the Seventh
Congressional District; July 31, 1846

The Single as Part of the Whole

It has been said that one bad general is better than two good ones, and the saying is true if taken to mean no more than that an army is better directed by a single mind, though inferior, than by two superior ones at variance and cross-purposes with each other.

—Message to Congress;
December 3, 1861

I go for all sharing the privileges of the government, who assist in bearing its burdens.

—Letter to the Editor of the Sangamo Journal;
June 13, 1836

Whatever I can I will do to protect you; meanwhile you must do your utmost to protect yourselves.

—Letter to Governor Murphy; April 27, 1864

The man of the highest moral cultivation, in spite of all which abstract principle can do, likes him whom he does know, much better than him whom he does not know. To correct the evils, great and small, which spring from want of sympathy, and from positive enmity, among strangers, as nations, or as individuals, is one of the highest functions of civilization.

—Address to the Wisconsin State Fair;
September 30, 1859

And the same is true in all joint operations wherein those engaged can have none but a common end in view and can differ only as to the choice of means. In a storm at sea no one on board can wish the ship to sink, and yet not unfrequently all go down together because too many will direct and no single mind can be allowed to control.

—Message to Congress;
December 3, 1861

Humility and Credit to Others

I must, in candor, say I do not think myself fit for the Presidency.

—Letter to T. J. Pickett;
April 16, 1859

In telling this tale, I attempt no compliment to my own sagacity. I claim not to have controlled events, but confess plainly that events have controlled me. Now, at the end of three years' struggle, the nation's condition is not what either party, or any man, devised or expected. God alone can claim it. Whither it is tending seems plain. If God now wills the removal of a great wrong, and wills also that we of the North, as well as you of the South, shall pay fairly for our complicity in that wrong, impartial history will find therein new cause to attest and revere the justice and goodness of God.

—Letter to A. G. Hodges;
April 4, 1864

Do not lean a hair's breadth against your own feelings, or your judgment of the public service, on the idea of gratifying me.

—Letter to Maj. Gen. Meade;
July 27, 1863

Calling to mind that we are in Baltimore, we cannot fail to note that the world moves. Looking upon these many people, assembled here, to serve, as they best may, the soldiers of the Union, it occurs at one that three years ago, the same soldiers could not so much as pass through Baltimore. The change from then till now, is both great, and gratifying. Blessings on the brave men who have wrought the change, and the fair women who strive to reward them for it.

—Address to the Sanitary Fair in Baltimore;
April 18, 1864

Let me assure you that I decline to be a candidate for Congress, on my clear conviction, that my running would hurt, & not help the cause. I am willing to make any personal sacrifice, but I am not willing to do, what in my own judgment, is, a sacrifice of the cause itself.

—Letter to Rev. J. M. Sturtevant;
September 27, 1856

CHAPTER 4

WORDS OF WISDOM FOR CONFLICT RESOLUTION

"Nothing through passion and ill temper."

On April 19, 1861, Private Luther Ladd became the first casualty of the Civil War. A seventeen–year–old mechanic from Massachusetts, Ladd had enlisted in the army with a sense of adventure and pro-Union patriotism. He was killed less than four days into his first mission when the citizens of Baltimore rioted as the 6th Massachusetts Infantry tried to make its way through the city to Camden train station. Within the next four years, over half a million enlisted soldiers would die; while thousands more Americans would become non-enlisted casualties of starvation, disease, suicide, and race-related violence.

In terms of lives lost, the Civil War remains the costliest military conflict in American history. Cities were burned, entire landscapes ransacked, and throughout it all there is ample evidence to suggest that Abraham Lincoln grieved deeply at the violence and bloodshed washing over the nation.

Numerous anecdotes exist about Lincoln's struggle to find peace in a nation at war. He was known for personally interceding when distraught widows wrote to him begging for a son to be discharged so the veteran could help support his siblings at home, or for a soldier's salary to be released when it was being withheld for some minor infraction. Lincoln's own bouts with "melancholia" are well documented, and his sadness and frustration at the massive loss of life is at the forefront of his writings during his years in the White House.

Yet equally as obvious as Lincoln's pain is his determination to rebuild and create a stronger nation. Throughout Lincoln's legal and political career he sought to find resolution—to create compromises that would allow opposing forces to each bend, but not break. In hindsight this characteristic lends itself to both criticism and praise. But as a leader in a time of crisis, Abraham Lincoln drew strength as a man of a select few absolutes. In those principles that he held sacred, Lincoln was as unyielding as granite; he was willing to pursue every means necessary to save the Union. At the same time, he was a leader who chose to look beyond his own ambition to envision a nation where Americans would have to live together after this great conflict had finally ended. He tempered determination with compassion, and endurance with flexibility. Though he would never live to see the Union he fought so valiantly for, Lincoln's steady guidance provided a framework for Americans to build peace upon long after his death.

Passionately Pursue Peace

It is always magnanimous to recant whatever we may have said in passion.

—Letter to William Butler;
February 1, 1839

We are not enemies, but friends. We must not be enemies. Though passion may have strained, it must not break our bonds of affection. The mystic chords of memory, stretching from every battle-field and patriot grave to every living heart and hearthstone all over this broad land, will yet swell the chorus of the

Union when again touched, as surely they will be, by the better angels of our nature.

—Lincoln's first Inaugural Address;
March 4, 1861

Persuade your neighbors to compromise whenever you can . . . As a peacemaker the lawyer has a superior opportunity of being a good man.

—Fragment; written circa July 1850

Can we not come together, for the future? Let everyone who really believes, and is resolved, that free society is not, and shall not be, a failure, and who can conscientiously declare that in the past contest he has done only what he thought best—let everyone have charity to believe that every other one can say as much. Thus let bygones be bygones. Let past differences, as nothing be; and with steady eye on the real issue, let us reinaugurate the good old "central ideas" of the Republic.

—Speech at the Republican banquet in Chicago;
December 10, 1856

Let us discard all this quibbling about this man and the other man, this race and that race and the other race being inferior and therefore they must be placed in an inferior position. Let us discard all these things, and unite as one people throughout this land, until we shall once more stand up declaring that all men are created equal.

—Reply to Stephen Douglas; July 10, 1858

Forgiveness without Compromise

I have desired as sincerely as any man, I sometimes think more than any other man, that our present difficulties might be settled without the shedding of blood.

—Address to the Frontier Guard;
April 26, 1861

Fondly do we hope, fervently do we pray, that this mighty scourge of war may speedily pass away. Yet, if God wills that it continue until all the wealth piled by the bondsman's two hundred and fifty years of unrequited toil shall be sunk, and until every drop of blood drawn by the lash shall be paid by another drawn with the sword, as was said three thousand years ago, so still it must be said, "The judgments of the Lord are true and righteous altogether." With malice toward none; with charity for all; with firmness in the right, as God gives us to see the right, let us strive on to finish the work we are in; to bind up the nation's wounds; to care for him who shall have borne the battle, and for his widow, and his orphan—to do all which may achieve and cherish a just and lasting peace among ourselves, and with all nations.

—Lincoln's second Inaugural Address;
March 4, 1865

I have here stated my purpose according to my views of official duty, and I intend no modification of my oft-expressed personal wish that all men everywhere could be free.

—Letter to Horace Greeley; August 22, 1862

The man does not live who is more devoted to peace than I am. None who would do more to preserve it. But it may be necessary to put the foot down firmly.

—Speech to the New Jersey General Assembly;
February 21, 1861

I don't want to quarrel with him—to call him a liar; but when I come square up to him I don't know what else to call him if I must tell the truth out. I want to be at peace, and reserve all my fighting powers for necessary occasions. My time is now very nearly out, and I give up the trifle that is left to the Judge, to let him set my knees trembling again, if he can.

—Reply to Stephen Douglas; September 15, 1858

Our popular government has often been called an experiment. Two points in it our people have already settled, the successful establishing and the successful administering of it. One still remains, its successful maintenance against a formidable internal attempt to overthrow it. It is now for them to demonstrate to the world that those who can fairly carry an election can also suppress a rebellion; that ballots are the rightful and peaceful successors of bullets; and that when ballots have fairly and constitutionally decided, there can be no successful appeal back to bullets; that there can be no successful appeal, except to ballots themselves, at succeeding elections. Such will be a great lesson of peace; teaching men that what they cannot take by an election, neither can they take by a war; teaching all the folly of being the beginners of a war.

—Message to Congress;
July 4, 1861

There is no line, straight or crooked, suitable for a national boundary, upon which to divide.

—Message to Congress;
December 1, 1862

Victory without Vengeance

I shall do nothing in malice. What I deal with is too vast for malicious dealing.

—Letter to Cuthbert Bullitt; July 28, 1862

Both read the same Bible, and pray to the same God; and each invokes His aid against the other. It may seem strange that any men should dare to ask a just God's assistance in wringing their bread from the sweat of other men's faces; but let us judge not that we be not judged. The prayers of both could not be answered; that of neither has been answered fully.

—Lincoln's second Inaugural Address;
March 4, 1865

There is no grievance that is a fit object of redress by mob law.

—Speech to the Young Men's Lyceum;
January 27, 1838

While we must, by all available means, prevent the overthrow of the government, we should avoid planting and cultivating too many thorns in the bosom of society.

—Letter to Edwin M. Stanton; March 18, 1864

Let us at all times remember that all American citizens are brothers of a common country, and should dwell together in the bonds of fraternal feeling.

—Speech at Springfield, Illinois;
November 20, 1860

When men take it in their heads today, to hang gamblers, or burn murderers, they should recollect, that, in the confusion usually attending such transactions, they will be as likely to hang or burn some one, who is neither a gambler nor a murderer as one who is; and that, acting upon the example they set, the mob of tomorrow, may, and probably will, hang or burn some of them, by the very same mistake.

—Speech to the Young Men's Lyceum;
January 27, 1838

But the election, along with its incidental, and undesirable strife, has done good too. It has demonstrated that a people's government can sustain a national election, in the midst of a great civil war. Until now it has not been known to the world that this was a possibility. It shows also how sound, and how strong we still are. It shows that, even among candidates of the same party, he who is most devoted to the Union, and most opposed to treason, can receive most of the people's votes. It shows also, to the extent yet known, that we have more men now, than we had when the war began.

—Reply to a spontaneous serenade;
November 10, 1864

It is exceedingly desirable that all parts of this great confederacy shall be at peace, and in harmony, one with another. Let us Republicans do our part to have it so. Even though much provoked, let us do nothing through passion and ill temper. Even though the Southern people will not so much as listen to us, let us calmly consider their demands, and yield to them if, in our deliberate view of our duty, we possibly can.

—Address at Cooper Institute; February 27, 1860

The severest justice may not always be the best policy.

—Veto message; July 17, 1862

I have not heard near so much upon that subject as you probably suppose; and I am slow to listen to criminations among friends, and never expose their quarrels on either side. My sincere wish is that both sides will allow bygones to be bygones, and look to the present and future only.

—Letter to unknown; August 31, 1860

Human nature will not change. In any future great national trial, compared with the men of this, we shall have as weak and as strong, as silly and as wise, as bad and as good. Let us, therefore, study the incidents of this as philosophy to learn wisdom from, and none of them as wrongs to be revenged.

—Reply to a spontaneous serenade;
November 10, 1864

To Build a New Future without Forgetting the Past

I distrust the wisdom if not the sincerity of friends who would hold my hands while my enemies stab me.

—Letter to Reverdy Johnson;
July 26, 1862

And then there will be some black men who can remember that with silent tongue, and clenched teeth, and steady eye, and well-poised bayonet, they have helped mankind on to this great consummation, while I fear there will be some white ones unable to forget that with malignant heart and deceitful speech they strove to hinder it.

—Letter to James C. Conkling;
August 26, 1863

If we reject and spurn them, we do our utmost to disorganize and disperse them. We, in effect, say to the white man: You are worthless or worse; we will neither help you, nor be helped by you. To the blacks, we say: This cup of liberty, which these, your old masters, hold to your lips, we will dash from you, and leave you to the chances of gathering the spilled and scattered contents in some vague and undefined when, where, and how. If this course, discouraging and paralyzing both white and black, has any tendency to bring Louisiana into proper, practical relations with the Union, I have so far been unable to perceive it. If, on the contrary, we recognize and sustain the new government . . . the converse of all this is made true. We encourage the hearts and nerve the arms of twelve thousand to adhere to their work, and argue for it, and proselyte for it, and fight for it, and feed it, and grow it, and ripen it to a complete success. The colored man, too, in seeing all united for him, is inspired with vigilance, and energy, and daring to the same end.

—Lincoln's last public address;
April 11, 1865

In your hands, my dissatisfied fellow-countrymen, and not in mine, is the momentous issue of civil war. The Government will not assail you. You can have no conflict without being yourselves the aggressors. You have no oath registered in heaven to destroy the

Government, while I shall have the most solemn one to "preserve, protect, and defend it."

—Lincoln's first Inaugural Address;
March 4, 1861

Our Republican robe is soiled and trailed in the dust. Let us purify it. Let us turn and wash it white in the spirit if not the blood of the Revolution. Let us turn slavery from its claims of moral right, back upon its existing legal rights and its arguments of necessity. Let us return it to the position our fathers gave it, and there let it rest in peace. Let us re-adopt the Declaration of Independence, and with it the practices and policy which harmonize with it. Let North and South, let all Americans, let all lovers of liberty everywhere, join in the great and good work. If we do this, we shall not only have saved the Union, but we shall have so saved it as to make and to keep it forever worthy of the saving.

—Reply to Stephen Douglas;
October 16, 1854

On principle I dislike an oath which requires a man to swear he has not done wrong. It rejects the Christian principle of forgiveness on terms of repentance. I think it is enough if the man does no wrong hereafter.

—Note to the Secretary of War; February 5, 1864

Strength and Flexibility

Exercise your own judgment, and do right for the public interest. Let your military measures be strong enough to repel the invader and keep the peace, and not so strong as to unnecessarily harass and persecute the people. It is a difficult role, and so much greater will be the honor if you perform it well. If both factions, or neither, shall abuse you, you will probably be about right. Beware of being assailed by one, and praised by the other.

> —Letter to Gen. J. M. Schofield;
> May 27, 1863

Yield larger things to which you can show no more than equal right; and yield lesser ones, though clearly your own. Better give your path to a dog, than be bitten by him in contesting for the right. Even killing the dog would not cure the bite.

> —Letter to Capt. James M. Cutts;
> October 26, 1863

Admitting Mistakes

My dear General, I do not remember that you and I ever met personally. I write this now as a grateful acknowledgment for the almost inestimable service you have done the country. I wish to say a word further. When you first reached the vicinity of Vicksburg . . . I never had any faith, except a general hope that you knew better than I. . . . When you got below and took Port Gibson, Grand Gulf, and vicinity and when you turned northward, east of the Big Black, I feared it was a mistake. I now wish to make the personal acknowledgment that you were right and I was wrong.

—Letter to Gen. Grant;
July 13, 1863

CHAPTER 5

DETERMINATION IN THE DARKEST HOURS

"The result is not doubtful. We shall not fail."

The weather in Washington D.C. on March 4, 1861 was oddly prophetic. A sunny dawn held the promise of a bright spring day, but by mid-morning ominous clouds had moved in to cast shadows over a still unfinished Capitol Building. Unperturbed by the blustery conditions, Abraham Lincoln donned his new, silk-lined stovepipe hat and drove in an open carriage down Pennsylvania Avenue. Once the wheels stopped, the president-elect unfolded himself from his seat and walked up to the Inauguration platform where he remained still until called forth to read his first Inaugural Address. Minutes later, he was sworn into office.

The presidential oath of office has remained unchanged since George Washington first took office in 1789. It is thirty-five words long, and can be spoken with perfect elocution in less than a minute. Abraham Lincoln was not the first, nor the last man to utter this single sentence; but he remains the only man whose presidential oath would be tested in the streets of America's cities and in the backyards of its citizens.

Throughout Lincoln's White House years, he endured political scandals, military defeats, personal loss, and a nation in crisis. As a leader he was wise enough to listen to doubts and bold enough to question his own policies. Yet most importantly, he was strong enough to endure.

At a time of staggering loss and constant change, Abraham Lincoln became a rock upon which Americans could either spit their venom or build their hopes. Even in the darkest times, Lincoln managed to pair brutal honesty with empathetic hope. Lincoln was a leader who did not hide behind false security, when those he was responsible to deserved truth. Even when grim circumstances presented nothing but a bleak future, the sixteenth president was a man capable of understanding desperate reality, and inspiring a nation to fight on regardless.

Hope as the Strongest Weapon

The power of hope upon human exertion and happiness is wonderful.

—Fragment; written circa July 1854

Let us hope, rather, that by the best cultivation of the physical world, beneath and around us; and the intellectual and moral world within us, we shall secure an individual, social, and political prosperity and happiness, whose course shall be onward and upward, and which, while the earth endures, shall not pass away.

—Address at the Wisconsin State Fair; September 30, 1859

In a word, the people will save their government, if the government itself will do its part only indifferently well.

—Message to Congress; July 8, 1861

We can do it. The human heart is with us—God is with us. We shall again be able not to declare, that "all states as states, are equal," nor yet that "all citizens as citizens are equal," but to renew the broader, better declaration, including both these and much more, that "all men are created equal."

—Speech at the Republican banquet in Chicago;
December 10, 1856

We simply must begin with and mould from disorganized and discordant elements.

—Lincoln's last public address;
April 11, 1865

Peace does not appear so distant as it did. I hope it will come soon, and come to stay; and so come as to be worth the keeping in all future time. It will then have been proved that among freemen there can be no successful appeal from the ballot to the bullet, and that they who take such appeal are sure to lose their case and pay the cost. . . . Still, let us not be over-sanguine of a speedy, final triumph. Let us be quite sober. Let us diligently apply the means, never doubting that a just God, in His own good time, will give us the rightful result.

—Letter to James C. Conkling; August 26, 1863

No one, not in my situation can appreciate my feeling of sadness at this parting. To this place, and the kindness of these people, I owe everything. Here I have lived a quarter of a century, and have passed from a young to an old man. Here my children have been born, and one is buried. I now leave, not knowing when, or whether ever, I may return, with a task before me greater than that which rested upon Washington. Without the assistance of that Divine Being, who ever attended him, I cannot succeed. With that assistance I cannot fail. Trusting in Him, who can go with me, and remain with you and be everywhere for good, let us confidently hope that all will yet be well.

—Speech at Great Western Railway;
February 11, 1861

Since your last annual assembling, another year of health and bountiful harvests has passed; and while it has not pleased the Almighty to bless us with a return of peace, we can but press on, guided by the best light He gives us, trusting that in His own good time and wise way, all will yet be well.

—Message to Congress; December 1, 1862

Know When to Ask for Help

The proportions of this rebellion were not for a long time understood. I saw that it involved the greatest difficulties, and would call forth all the powers of the whole country.

—Reply to Members of the Presbyterian General Assembly; June 2, 1863

If all do not join now to save the good old ship of the Union this voyage, nobody will have a chance to pilot her on another voyage.

—Speech at Cleveland, Ohio; February 15, 1861

I beg you to remember this, not merely for my sake, but for yours. I happen temporarily to occupy this big White House. I am a living witness that any one of your children may look to come here as my father's child has. It is in order that each of you may have through this free government which we have enjoyed, an open field and a fair chance for your industry, enterprise and intelligence; that you may all have equal privileges in the race of life, with all its desirable human aspirations. It is for this the struggle should be maintained, that we may not lose our birthright—not only for one, but for two or three years. The nation is worth fighting for, to secure such an inestimable jewel.

—Address to the 166th Ohio Regiment; August 22, 1864

Where there is a Will, There is a Way

And by the successful, and the unsuccessful, let it be remembered, that while occasions like the present, bring their sober and durable benefits, the exultations and mortifications of them are but temporary; that the victor shall soon be the vanquished, if he relax in his exertion; and that the vanquished this year, may be victor the next, in spite of all competition.

—Address at the Wisconsin State Fair;
September 30, 1859

Many free countries have lost their liberty, and ours may lose hers; but if she shall, be it my proudest plume, not that I was the last to desert, but that I never deserted her. I know that the great volcano at Washington, aroused and directed by the evil spirit that reigns there, is belching forth the lava of political corruption in a current broad and deep, which is sweeping with frightful velocity over the whole length and breadth of the land, bidding fair to leave unscathed no green spot or living thing; while on its bosom are riding, like demons on the waves of hell, the imps of that evil spirit, and fiendishly taunting all those who dare resist its destroying course with the hopelessness of their effort; and, knowing this, I cannot deny that all may be swept away. Broken by it

I, too, may be; bow to it I never will. The probability that we may fall in the struggle ought not to deter us from the support of a cause we believe to be just; it shall not deter me. If ever I feel the soul within me elevate and expand to those dimensions not wholly unworthy of its almighty Architect, it is when I contemplate the cause of my country deserted by all the world beside, and I standing up boldly and alone, and hurling defiance at her victorious oppressors. Here, without contemplating consequences, before high heaven and in the face of the world, I swear eternal fidelity to the just cause, as I deem it, of the land of my life, my liberty, and my love. And who that thinks with me will not fearlessly adopt the oath that I take? Let none falter who thinks he is right, and we may succeed.

—Speech given at the House of Representatives at Springfield, Illinois; December 20, 1839

The fight must go on. The cause of civil liberty must not be surrendered at the end of one, or even one hundred defeats.

—Letter to Henry Asbury; November 19, 1858

Two years ago the Republicans of the nation mustered over thirteen hundred thousand strong. We did this under the single impulse of resistance to a common danger, with every external circumstance against us.

Of strange, discordant, and even, hostile elements, we gathered from the four winds, and formed and fought the battle through, under the constant hot fire of a disciplined, proud, and pampered enemy. Did we brave all then, to falter now?—now—when that same enemy is wavering, dissevered and belligerent? The result is not doubtful. We shall not fail—if we stand firm, we shall not fail.

—Speech at the Republican Convention;
June 16, 1858

I have seen your dispatch expressing your unwillingness to break your hold where you are. Neither am I willing. Hold on with a bull-dog grip, and chew & choke, as much as possible.

—Letter to Gen. Grant; August 17, 1864

I expect to maintain this contest until successful, or till I die, or am conquered, or my term expires, or Congress or the country forsakes me.

—Letter to William H. Seward; June 28, 1862

Focus and You Shall Not Falter

"Must" is the word.

—Letter to George C. Latham;
July 22, 1860

And having thus chosen our course, without guile, and with pure purpose, let us renew our trust in God, and go forward without fear, and with manly hearts.

—Message to Congress;
July 4, 1861

We can succeed only by concert. It is not "Can any of us imagine better?" but "Can we all do better?"

—Message to Congress;
December 1, 1862

We have to fight this battle upon principle, and upon principle alone. I am, in a certain sense, made the standard-bearer in behalf of the Republicans. I was made so merely because there had to be some one so placed—I being in no wise, preferable to any other one of the twenty-five—perhaps a hundred we have in the Republican ranks. Then I say I wish it to be distinctly understood and borne in mind, that we have to fight this battle without many—perhaps without any—of the external aids which are brought to bear against us. So I hope those with whom I am surrounded have principle enough to nerve themselves for the task and leave nothing undone, that can be fairly done, to bring about the right result.

—Reply to Stephen Douglas;
July 17, 1858

Gen. Sheridan says "If the thing is pressed I think that Lee will surrender." Let the thing be pressed.

—Letter to Gen. Grant;
April 7, 1865

A Battle is Lost, But the War Can Still be Won

Wise counsels may accelerate it, or mistakes may delay it but, sooner or later, the victory is sure to come.

—Speech at the Republican Convention;
June 16, 1858

DEAR SIR:—Yours of the 13th was received some days ago. The fight must go on. The cause of civil liberty must not be surrendered at the end of one or even one hundred defeats. Douglas had the ingenuity to be supported in the late contest both as the best means to break down and to uphold the slave interest. No ingenuity can keep these antagonistic elements in harmony long. Another explosion will soon come.

—Letter to H. Asbury; November 19, 1858

I am older than you, have felt badly myself, and know, what I tell you is true. Adhere to your purpose and you will soon feel as well as you ever did. On the contrary, if you falter, and give up, you will lose the power of keeping any resolution, and will regret it all your life.

—Letter to Quintin Campbell; June 28, 1862

MY DEAR SIR:—I expect the result of the election went hard with you. So it did with me, too, perhaps not quite so hard as you may have supposed. I have an abiding faith that we shall beat them in the long run. Step by step the objects of the leaders will become too plain for the people to stand them. I write merely to let you know that I am neither dead nor dying. Please give my respects to your good family, and all inquiring friends.

—Letter to A. Sympson; December 12, 1858

I believe, according to a letter of yours to Hatch, you are "feeling like h—ll yet." Quit that—you will soon feel better. Another "blow up" is coming; and we shall have fun again.

—Letter to Dr. C. H. Ray; November 20, 1858

Strength in the Bleakest of Moments

But if, after all, we shall fail, be it so. We still shall have the proud consolation of saying to our consciences, and to the departed shade of our country's freedom, that the cause approved of our judgment, and adored of our hearts, in disaster, in chains, in torture, in death, we never faltered in defending.

—Speech given at the House of Representatives at Springfield, Illinois; December 20, 1839

I think we have fairly entered upon a durable struggle as to whether this nation is to ultimately become all slave or all free, and though I fall early in the contest, it is nothing if I shall have contributed, in the least degree, to the final rightful result.

—Letter to H. D. Sharpe;
December 8, 1858

Dear Madam,

I have been shown in the files of the War Department a statement of the Adjutant General of Massachusetts that you are the mother of five sons who have died gloriously on the field of battle.

I feel how weak and fruitless must be any word of mine which should attempt to beguile you from the grief of a loss so overwhelming. But I cannot refrain from tendering you the consolation that may be found in the thanks of the Republic they died to save.

I pray that our Heavenly Father may assuage the anguish of your bereavement, and leave you only the cherished memory of the loved and lost, and the solemn pride that must be yours to have laid so costly a sacrifice upon the altar of freedom.

Yours, very sincerely and respectfully,
A. Lincoln

—Complete letter to Mrs. Lydia Bixby;
November 21, 1864

I have often inquired of myself, what great principle or idea it was that kept this confederacy so long together. It was not the mere matter of the separation of the colonies from the mother land; but something in that Declaration giving liberty, not alone to the people of this country, but hope to the world for all future time. It was that which gave promise that in due time the weights would be lifted from the shoulders of all men, and that all should have an equal chance. This is the sentiment embodied in the Declaration of Independence. Now, my friends, can this country be saved on that basis? If it can, I will consider myself one of the happiest men in the world if I can help to save it. If it cannot be saved upon that principle, it will be truly awful. But if this country cannot be saved without giving up that principle, I was about to say I would rather be assassinated on this spot than surrender it.

—Speech at Independence Hall; February 22, 1861

On the contrary, nobody has ever expected me to be President. In my poor, lean, lank face, nobody has ever seen that any cabbages were sprouting out. These are disadvantages, all taken together, that the Republicans labor under. We have to fight this battle upon principle, and upon principle alone.

—Speech at Springfield, Illinois; July 17, 1858

The struggle of today, is not altogether for today—it is for a vast future also. With a reliance on Providence, all the more firm and earnest, let us proceed in the great task which events have devolved upon us.

—Message to Congress; December 3, 1861

I know not how to aid you, save in the assurance of one of mature age, and much severe experience, that you cannot fail, if you resolutely determine, that you will not.

—Letter to George C. Latham; July 22, 1860

Of our political revolution of '76 we are all justly proud. It has given us a degree of political freedom far exceeding that of any other nation of the earth. In it the world has found a solution of the long-mooted problem as to the capability of man to govern himself. In it was the germ which has vegetated, and still is to grow and expand into the universal liberty of mankind. But, with all these glorious results, past, present, and to come, it had its evils too. It breathed forth famine, swam in blood, and rode in fire; and long, long after, the orphan's cry and the widow's wail continued to break the sad silence that ensued. These were the price, the inevitable price, paid for the blessings it bought. . . . And when the victory shall be complete, when there shall be neither a slave nor a drunkard on the earth, how proud the title of that land which may truly claim to be the birthplace and the cradle of both those revolutions that shall have ended in that victory. How nobly distinguished that people who shall have planted and nurtured to maturity both the political and moral freedom of their species.

—Address to the Washington Temperance Society; February 22, 1842

CHAPTER 6

ESSENTIAL READING: SELECTED QUOTES AND SPEECHES OF LINCOLN

There can be no doubt that Lincoln was a great leader, and that his words will continue to inspire generations to come. In this short book we have attempted to mine through the literary treasure trove of Lincoln's legacy for those few gems we felt best capture Lincoln's leadership lessons.

Yet, there are some statements—profound, humble, mundane, exceptional and more—that simply cannot be placed under any suitable heading. We hope that perhaps in this smattering of phrases below, readers will forge a unique connection with, and curiosity about, Abraham Lincoln.

Lincoln the Mere Man

If any personal description of me is thought desirable, it may be said I am, in height, six feet four inches, nearly; lean in flesh, weighing on an average one hundred and eighty pounds; dark complexion, with coarse black hair and gray eyes. No other marks or brands recollected.

—Letter to J. W. Fell; December 20, 1859

My dear little Miss, Your very agreeable letter of the 15th is received. I regret the necessity of saying I have no daughter. I have three sons—one seventeen, one nine, and one seven years of age. They, with their mother, constitute my whole family. As to the whiskers, having never worn any, do you not think people would call it a piece of silly affectation if I were to begin it now?

—Letter to Miss Grace Bedell;
October 19, 1860

How miserably things seem to be arrang.
world. If we have no friends, we have no pleasu.
and if we have them, we are sure to lose them, and be
doubly pained by the loss.

—Letter to Josiah Speed; February 25, 1842

Essential Reading

I say there is room enough for us all to be free.

—Speech at Cincinnati, Ohio; September 17, 1859

To the best of my judgment I have labored for, and
not against the Union.

—Speech at Springfield, Illinois; October 29, 1858

Understanding the spirit of our institutions to aim at
the elevation of men, I am opposed to whatever tends
to degrade them.

—Letter to Dr. Theodore Canisius; May 17, 1859

If A. can prove, however conclusively, that he may,
of right, enslave B. Why may not B. snatch the same
argument, and prove equally, that he may enslave A?
You say A. is white, and B. is black. It is color, then;
the lighter, having the right to enslave the darker?
Take care. By this rule, you are to be slave to the first

man you meet, with a fairer skin than your own. You do not mean color exactly?—You mean the whites are intellectually the superiors of the blacks, and, therefore have the right to enslave them? Take care again. By this rule, you are to be slave to the first man you meet, with an intellect superior to your own. But, you say, it is a question of interest; and, if you can make it your interest, you have the right to enslave another. Very well. And if he can make it his interest, he has the right to enslave you.

—Fragment; written circa July 1854

Our progress in degeneracy appears to me to be pretty rapid. As a nation, we began by declaring that all men are created equal. We now practically read it, all men are created equal except negroes. When the Know-nothings get control, it will read, all men are created equal except negroes and foreigners and Catholics. When it comes to this, I shall prefer emigrating to some country where they make no pretence of loving liberty—to Russia, for instance, where despotism can be taken pure, and without the base alloy of hypocrisy

—Letter to Joshua F. Speed; August 24, 1855

It is seventy-two years since the first inauguration of a President under our national Constitution. During that period fifteen different and greatly distinguished citizens have, in succession, administered the executive branch of the government. They have conducted it through many perils, and generally with great success. Yet, with all this scope of precedent, I now enter upon the same task for the brief Constitutional term of four years under great and peculiar difficulty. A disruption of the Federal Union, heretofore only menaced, is now formidably attempted. I hold that, in contemplation of universal law and of the Constitution, the Union of these States is perpetual. Perpetuity is implied, if not expressed, in the fundamental law of all national governments. It is safe to assert that no government proper ever had a provision in its organic law for its own termination. Continue to execute all the express provisions of our National Constitution, and the Union will endure forever—it being impossible to destroy it except by some action not provided for in the instrument itself.

—Lincoln's first Inaugural Address;
March 4, 1861

A nation may be said to consist of its territory, its people, and its laws. The territory is the only part which is of certain durability. "One generation passeth away and another generation cometh, but the earth abideth forever." It is of the first importance to duly consider and estimate this ever-enduring part.

—Message to Congress; December 1, 1862

What is conservatism? Is it not adherence to the old and tried, against the new and untried?

—Address at Cooper Institute; February 27, 1860

I believe the declaration that "all men are created equal" is the great fundamental principle upon which our free institutions rest; that negro slavery is violative of that principle.

—Letter to J. U. Brown; October 18, 1858

As each man has one mouth to be fed, and one pair of hands to furnish food, it was probably intended that that particular pair of hands should feed that particular mouth.

—Address at the Wisconsin State Fair; September 30, 1859

Considering the great degree of modesty which should always attend youth, it is probable I have already been more presuming than becomes me.

—Open letter to the People of Sangamo County; March 9, 1832

Gold is good in its place, but living, brave, patriotic men are better than gold.

—Reply to a spontaneous serenade; November 10, 1864

This is the one hundred and tenth anniversary of the birthday of Washington; we are met to celebrate this day. Washington is the mightiest name of earth, long since mightiest in the cause of civil liberty, still mightiest in moral reformation. On that name no eulogy is expected. It cannot be. To add brightness to the sun or glory to the name of Washington is alike impossible. Let none attempt it. In solemn awe pronounce the name, and in its naked deathless splendor leave it shining on.

—Speech to the Washington Temperance Society;
February 22, 1842

The resources, advantages, and powers of the American people are very great, and they have consequently succeeded to equally great responsibilities. It seems to have devolved upon them to test whether a government established on the principles of human freedom can be maintained against an effort to build one upon the exclusive foundation of human bondage.

—Letter to the Working Men of London, England;
February 1, 1863

Thanks to all, for the great Republic, for the principle it lives by and keeps alive, for man's vast future, thanks to all.

—Letter to James C. Conkling; August 26, 1863

By the President of the United States of America:

A Proclamation.

Whereas, on the twenty-second day of September, in the year of our Lord one thousand eight hundred and sixty-two, a proclamation was issued by the President of the United States, containing, among other things, the following, to wit:

That on the first day of January, in the year of our Lord one thousand eight hundred and sixty-three, all persons held as slaves within any State or designated part of a State, the people whereof shall then be in rebellion against the United States, shall be then, thenceforward, and forever free; and the Executive Government of the United States, including the military and naval authority thereof, will recognize and maintain the freedom of such persons, and will do no act or acts to repress such persons, or any of them, in any efforts they may make for their actual freedom.

That the Executive will, on the first day of January aforesaid, by proclamation, designate the States and parts of States, if any, in which the people thereof, respectively, shall then be in rebellion against the United States; and the fact that any State, or the people thereof, shall on that day be, in good faith, represented in the Congress of the United States by members chosen thereto at elections wherein a majority of the qualified voters of such State shall have participated, shall, in the absence of strong countervailing testimony, be deemed conclusive evidence that such State, and the people thereof, are not then in rebellion against the United States.

Now, therefore I, Abraham Lincoln, President of the United States, by virtue of the power in me vested as Commander-in-Chief, of the Army and Navy of the United States in time of actual armed rebellion against the authority and government of the United States, and as a fit and necessary war measure for suppressing said rebellion, do, on this first day of January, in the year of our Lord one thousand eight hundred and sixty-three, and in accordance with my purpose so to do publicly proclaimed for the full period of one hundred days, from the day first above mentioned, order and designate as the States and parts of States wherein the people thereof respectively, are this day in rebellion against the United States, the following, to wit:

Arkansas, Texas, Louisiana, (except the Parishes of St. Bernard, Plaquemines, Jefferson, St. John, St. Charles, St. James Ascension, Assumption, Terrebonne, Lafourche, St. Mary, St. Martin, and Orleans, including the City of New Orleans) Mississippi, Alabama, Florida, Georgia,

South Carolina, North Carolina, and Virginia, (except the forty—eight counties designated as West Virginia, and also the counties of Berkley, Accomac, Northampton, Elizabeth City, York, Princess Ann, and Norfolk, including the cities of Norfolk and Portsmouth[]], and which excepted parts, are for the present, left precisely as if this proclamation were not issued.

And by virtue of the power, and for the purpose aforesaid, I do order and declare that all persons held as slaves within said designated States, and parts of States, are, and henceforward shall be free; and that the Executive government of the United States, including the military and naval authorities thereof, will recognize and maintain the freedom of said persons.

And I hereby enjoin upon the people so declared to be free to abstain from all violence, unless in necessary self-defence; and I recommend to them that, in all cases when allowed, they labor faithfully for reasonable wages.

And I further declare and make known, that such persons of suitable condition, will be received into the armed service of the United States to garrison forts, positions, stations, and other places, and to man vessels of all sorts in said service.

And upon this act, sincerely believed to be an act of justice, warranted by the Constitution, upon military necessity, I invoke the considerate judgment of mankind, and the gracious favor of Almighty God.

In witness whereof, I have hereunto set my hand and caused the seal of the United States to be affixed.

Done at the City of Washington, this first day of January, in the year of our Lord one thousand eight hundred and sixty three, and of the Independence of the United States of America the eighty-seventh.

By the President:
ABRAHAM LINCOLN
WILLIAM H. SEWARD,
Secretary of State.

LIST OF WORKS CITED

Angle, Paul M., and Earl Schenck Miers. *The Living Lincoln: The Man, His Mind, His Times, and the War He Fought, Reconstructed from His Own Writings.* New York: Barnes and Noble Books, 1992.

Lincoln, Abraham. *Speeches and Letters of Abraham Lincoln: 1832-1865.* Merwin Roe, Ed. New York: E. P. Dutton & Co, 1912.

Lincoln, Abraham. *The Papers And Writings Of Abraham Lincoln, Complete Constitutional Edition.* Arthur Brooks Lapsley, Ed. as accessed from www .gutenberg.org on July 18, 2011.

Sandburg, Carl. *Abraham Lincoln: The Prairie Years and The War Years.* One-Volume Ed. San Diego: Harcourt, Inc., 1982.

"Government, even in its best state, is but a necessary evil; in its worst state, an intolerable one."
—*Thomas Paine*

Thomas Paine on Liberty
Including *Common Sense* and Other Writings
Thomas Paine

Thomas Paine is most famous for writing *Common Sense,* a pamphlet distributed during the American Revolution advocating for colonial America's independence from Great Britain. Now, collected here in a beautiful gift book volume are excerpts from this important historical American document, as well as several of his other writings.

Paine believed in more than just freedom in the form of revolution and overthrowing governments. He also believed in freedom from oppressive and organized religions and monopolies. Included in this book are passages taken from The Age of Reason and The Rights of Man, as well as letters to George Washington, Benjamin Rush, and Samuel Adams, and pamphlets such as "The American Crisis" and "Agrarian Justice." Throughout his writings, Paine provides excellent and timeless wisdom on attaining liberty and living a democratic life.

$9.95 Hardcover • 144 pages

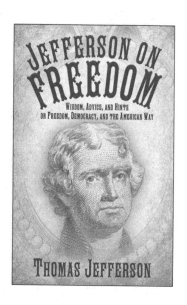

Jefferson on Freedom
Wisdom, Advice, and Hints on Freedom, Democracy, and the American Way
Thomas Jefferson

Thomas Jefferson is most famous for the writing of the Declaration of Independence, which espouses the general principles of freedom and democracy that Americans hold dear. Now, collected here for the first time, is this historical American document, as well as several of his other famous writings. Included in this book are excerpts from his only full-length book, *Notes on the State of Virginia*, letters to Samual Kercheval and Edward Carrington on liberal democracy and freedom, an exchange with Danbury Baptists regarding the right to religious freedom, and his manual on parliamentary policy. Jefferson provides excellent and timeless quotes on attaining freedom and living a democratic life.

$9.95 Hardcover • 144 pages

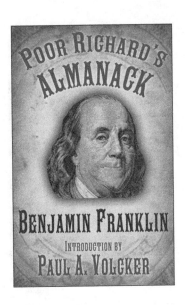

Poor Richard's Almanack
Benjamin Franklin
Introduction by Paul A. Volcker

Benjamin Franklin's classic book is full of timeless, thought-provoking insights that are as valuable today as they were over two centuries ago. With more than 700 pithy proverbs, Franklin lays out the rules everyone should live by and offers advice on such subjects as money, friendship, marriage, ethics, and human nature. They range from the famous "A penny saved is a penny earned" to the lesser-known but equally practical "When the wine enters, out goes the truth." Other truisms like "Fish and visitors stink after three days" combine sharp wit with wisdom. Paul Volcker's new introduction offers a fascinating perspective on Franklin's beloved work.

$9.95 Hardcover • 96 pages

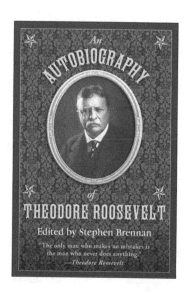

An Autobiography of Theodore Roosevelt
Edited by Stephen Brennan

Based in part on his own writings, this is the true story of one of America's most beloved leaders. From president of the board of New York City Police Commissioners, secretary of the Navy, founder of the Rough Riders during the war with Cuba, his time as the governor of New York, to vice president and eventually, after the assignation of President McKinley, becoming the twenty-sixth president of the United States, Theodore Roosevelt's role in the shaping of the United States is still felt today. Illustrated with drawings and photos, discover the rich history of this great man's life here.

$12.95 Hardcover • 400 pages

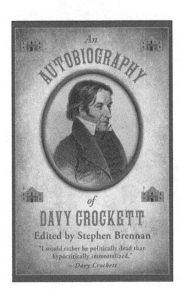

An Autobiography of Davy Crockett
Edited by Stephen Brennan

Based in part on Davy Crockett's own writings, this is the true story of one of America's most iconic historical figures. From his days as a scout for Andrew Jackson during the war of 1812, his time as a congressman for the state of Tennessee, and his eventual death at the Alamo, Davy Crockett led a life that was admired and idealized by people all across America, to this very day. Read about the monopolist and corporate misdeeds, environmental degradation, and foreign military adventures that he battled during his amazing life. Illustrated with drawings and photos, discover the rich history—part myth and part fact—behind this great American man.

$12.95 Hardcover • 320 pages